VEGETARIAN PLEASURES

Healthy Cooking for Sharing & Celebration

KAREN MANGUM, M.S., R.D.

BON VIVANT

BON VIVANT PRESS • MONTEREY, CALIFORNIA

Front cover photography by Robert N. Fish
Back cover photography by Stan Sinclair
Interior photography by Sinclair Studio, Inc.
Edited by Bonnie Widicker
Designed by Linda Griffith Criswell & Tim Larson
Food styling by Rebecca Robison
Typesetting by Mark Winchester

Library of Congress Cataloging-in-Publication Data

Mangum, Karen
Vegetarian Pleasures, Fine Vegetarian Cooking for
Sharing and Celebration

ISBN   1-883214-18-1

CIP   97-073972

Includes indexes
Autobiography page

Published by Bon Vivant Press
an imprint of the Millennium Publishing Group
PO Box 1994
Monterey, CA 93942

Printed in Hong Kong

What Others Are Saying About Vegetarian Pleasures— Fine Vegetarian Cooking For Sharing & Celebration

Finally, a vegetarian cookbook like no other...This one cookbook will allow me to toss all of my other cookbooks. — *Small Press Magazine*

A beautiful cookbook with outstanding photographs and even more outstanding recipes...there's nothing bland about these recipes. Thoughtful commentary contributes to its warmth. — *The Culinary Sleuth*

You'll find serious good cooking and terrific ideas in this collection. — *Cooking Light Magazine's Top Ten Cookbook List*

Mangum has created a vegetarian book that displays food you actually want to try. There are more than 60 glossy, beautiful photographs and lovely, simple surprises. — *Orange County Register*

A fresh look at vegetarian cookery, with 140 imaginative, healthful recipes. — *Dallas Times Herald*

This cookbook is posh with lovely photographs of fruits and vegetables and "real-people" recipes. Dishes are nicely seasoned. — *Chicago Sun-Times*

Mangum gives meatless meals a good name. Her friendly new book offers good-tasting, great-looking vegetarian dishes for all seasons. — *Toronto Sun*

One of the prettiest, most delicious cookbooks of the season. You'll hardly notice that there are no recipes for meat. — *Fresno Bee*

C O N T E N T S

Foreword   7
How It All Came to Be   9
Introduction   10
How to Use This Book   11

SPRING
    I Love You's   15
    New Beginnings   22
    Rainy Days   27
    Blooms of the Season   33
    Kites and Kittens   37
    Mother's Lap   43

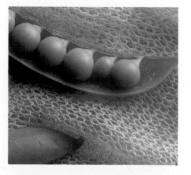

SUMMER
    Legacies   49
    Midsummer Night's Dream   53
    Under the Stars   60
    Glorious Gardens   65
    Freedom   69
    Fiesta and Siesta   75

AUTUMN
    Back to School   81
    Football Weather   85
    Changing Colors   89
    Celebrating the Harvest   93
    For Papa   98
    Family Gatherings   103

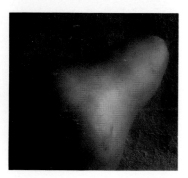

WINTER

    Congratulations Are in Order   110

    Firelight Warmth   115

    Unexpected Guests   120

    Cocooning   125

    Winter Workouts   130

    Home for the Holidays   136

Healthful Gifts of Good Taste   143

A Matter of Fat   144

Menu Makeover   145

Feasting on Fiber   146

Grazing on Grains   147

Glossary of Greens   148

Living on Legumes   149

Complementary Proteins   150

Grocery Guide   151

Index of Recipes   154

Index of Ingredients   156

DEDICATION

To my mother, Ruth Clifford, whose
tremendous cooking talent has inspired me throughout my
life, and to my husband, Michael, and our four children
for their patience and willingness to try
"something new."

HOW IT ALL CAME TO BE

As soon as people taste recipes from *Vegetarian Pleasures* and hear that I am a Registered Dietitian and recipe developer, they often ask, "Can you come to my house and fix meals for my family?" They picture a daily dose of full-course dinners consisting of delicious and nutritious dishes followed by an equally fabulous dessert, all effortlessly prepared and lavishly garnished. They figure that if a food-nutrition professional can't do it, who can? Well, the truth is, I can't do it and I don't know anybody else who does it (besides my mother, but that was a different generation). My life is as harried and hectic as anybody else's. I'm the busy mother of four children, a recipe developer, cooking instructor, PTA volunteer and on and on. With all the time I spend with and around food, often the last thing I want to do is cook. When I'm not calling for take-out, I prepare recipes that are simple and healthful with three-star taste.

I wrote *Vegetarian Pleasures* for people like me – those with a desire for nutritious choices and sophisticated palates, but who haven't time to fuss. If we are not totally vegetarian, we are adding more meatless meals to our repertoire. We may be single, married with children, or without, but we share a common goal of eating nutritious, tasty, quick-to-fix meals.

Vegetarian Pleasures is a refreshing departure from most vegetarian cookbooks. Here's why:

❖ Sixty pages of spectacular food photography by award-winning photographer, Stan Sinclair, whet your appetite, and demonstrate what the recipe results can resemble.

❖ Recipes call for easy-to-find ingredients and simple cooking techniques requiring basic cooking equipment.

❖ Seasonal divisions guide your selection of recipes to assure ingredients will be at their best and freshest.

❖ Each season devotes six menus to the often-overlooked, simple pleasures of life which can be shared and celebrated with food, family and/or friends.

❖ Symbols direct you to those recipes taking 30 minutes or less to prepare.

❖ Nutrition analysis of each recipe helps you stick to your health goals.

Take a peek. *Vegetarian Pleasures* reassures us that food is pleasurable because it doesn't have to take hours to prepare tasty dishes and because we can share it with people who make life meaningful. Welcome and enjoy!

INTRODUCTION

Our life is frittered away by detail. . . . Simplify, simplify.
—HENRY DAVID THOREAU
1817-1862

The "slices of life" represented in this book describe moments that make my life much more pleasurable. These are simple pleasures, things I cannot see: relationships, feelings of security and love, tests of character, visual feasts of nature, milestones in our lives, plus health and vitality. These are my personal simple pleasures.

Consider health and vitality. Most of us take these pleasures for granted until illness and fatigue strike. But we have information available to help us keep healthy and vital. We are urged to simplify our dietary patterns by eating fewer processed foods, substituting more whole-grain foods for them. We are told to be more moderate in using fats and sugars and to include a variety of foods in our menus. It comes as no surprise that following these guidelines helps to protect us against diseases, including the major ones of heart disease, cancer, diabetes, obesity, and osteoporosis.

When reminded of these health-promoting guidelines, we protest that there just isn't time or it isn't convenient to fix truly healthful meals. Some say that it is impossible to prepare tasty, nutritious recipes in less than 30 minutes. I say, for health's sake, that we cannot afford to do otherwise. *Life's Simple Pleasures* was created to meet this need.

These are the guidelines that I used to select the recipes in this book.

Taste and Design: The recipes have been tested and tasted by me and by willing friends. It was an interesting task to select menus for color, shape, and design potential so that the foods look as fantastic as they taste.

Convenience: Most of the recipes in this book take 30 minutes or less to prepare from start to finish. These are identified by a symbol. Other recipes require additional time for chilling, baking, marinating. These also are identified by a symbol (see How to Use This Book). I have included numerous recipes that can be prepared ahead.

Low Fat: The United States Dietary Guidelines suggest cutting fat intake to 30 percent or less of daily calories. Because you will not always be making each menu in its entirety, I selected recipes with fat contents of about 30 percent or less. When a recipe's fat percentage exceeds that, I suggest you combine it with recipes of lower fat content, so that the total fat percentage of your menu meets the guidelines.

High Fiber: Healthful recipes emphasize the use of whole grains, along with fresh fruits and vegetables, with as little processing as possible. Be sure to read Feasting on Fiber and Grazing on Grains. Remember to work into a high-fiber diet gradually.

Vegetarian: New evidence shows that many diseases in the United States are strongly associated with our high consumption of animal fat. This book encourages you to replace meat protein with plant protein and to include low-fat dairy products so that you can maintain high-quality protein without the negative effects of animal fat (see Complementary Proteins and Living on Legumes).

H O W   T O   U S E   T H I S   B O O K

Menu Themes

The book is divided into the four seasons with six complete menus for each of these seasons.

Seasonal divisions alert you to times when foods, especially fresh produce, are at their best and at their most economical price. In most cases, a menu contains an appetizer or soup, main entree, salad, bread, and dessert. These recipes suit the chosen theme. Color, taste, and nutritional compatibility also were considered when creating these theme-appropriate menus.

Nutritional Analysis

A nutritional analysis (The Food Processor I, ESHA Research, Salem, Oregon) appears at the bottom of each recipe. Fractions are rounded to the nearest whole number. The number in parentheses, which appears after the listing of grams of fat, is the percentage of calories from fat. Optional ingredients have been included in the recipe analysis. Garnishes have not been included except when they add significant nutrients. The sodium levels are low because the amount of salt in most recipes has been left to your taste.

The nutrient analyses are *approximate* values for calories; grams of protein, carbohydrate, and fat; milligrams of cholesterol and sodium.

The nutritional information provided helps you make informed choices. Most of the recipes in the book are low in fat (less than 30 percent of calories from fat). I do not mean to imply that we should only eat foods that are this low in fat. The recipes were chosen because you are more likely to prepare selected recipes from a menu rather than the entire menu itself. Get in the habit of combining high- and low-fat foods so that your entire day's intake is below the 30 percent fat level. Selecting foods in this way allows you to choose from all kinds for moderation and balance.

Symbols

If you are in a hurry, look for recipes with these symbols identifying them as quick to fix:

    ♣ - total preparation time 30 minutes or less

    ❦ - preparation time 30 minutes or less, with additional time for baking, chilling, marinating

Photographs

The way a meal is presented adds a great deal to any eating experience. Sense of sight is powerful. I felt it was important to emphasize the visual impact of these recipes. As a result, beautiful photographs accompany each menu, visually describing the recipes. Take full advantage of the new ideas they offer you. You're invited to "break the rules" in order to turn the ordinary into something unique.

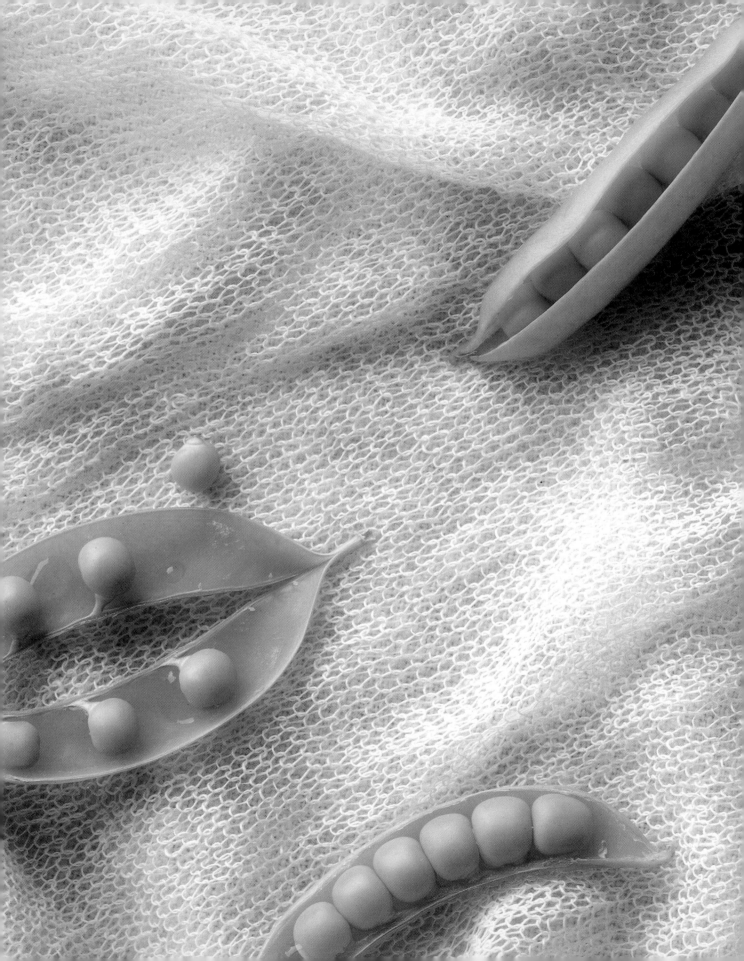

I Love You's

♣

Sweet Pea Pod Soup

This recipe uses a fresh sugar snap pea, which is a cross between the rounder shell pea and the flat snow pea. Buy the smallest pods for the sweetest flavor. Freshness is the key when buying any pea because, like corn, the sugar gradually turns to starch once it is picked. The best way to check for freshness is to snap open a pod and eat a pea. It should taste sweet.

- 3 tablespoons reduced-calorie margarine, divided
- 1 cup leeks, thinly sliced
- 2 tablespoons flour
- 1 (10-ounce) package frozen petite peas
- 4 cups Vegetable Broth (see p. 91)
- 1 pound fresh sugar snap peas or snow peas, strings removed
- 2 cups butter lettuce, chopped
- 1½ cups water
- ½ cup light cream
- ½ cup plain low-fat yogurt
- ❧ *garnish:* plain low-fat yogurt, butter lettuce, and green onions

In a heavy saucepan, melt 2 tablespoons margarine; add the leeks and sauté until tender (about 10 minutes). Add flour, mixing well. Stir in the frozen peas and broth. Cook for 20 minutes over low heat. Transfer the cooked mixture to food processor or electric blender. Purée. Set aside.

Cook the snap or snow peas and lettuce with the remaining 1 tablespoon margarine in the water for about 15 minutes. Purée this mixture in food processor or electric blender. Strain to remove any fibers.

Combine puréed mixtures and thin with the cream and yogurt. Add salt and pepper, if desired, to taste. Garnish with a dollop of yogurt, sliced butter lettuce, and green onions.

Serves 8
Per 1 cup serving: 128 calories, 8 grams protein, 14 grams carbohydrate, 5 grams fat (32%), 7 milligrams cholesterol, 459 milligrams sodium.

M·E·N·U

Sweet Pea Pod Soup

•

*Blushing Pink on Tender Greens &
Grapefruit Vinaigrette*

•

Broccoli & Cheese Quiche

•

Honey-Peach Bran Muffins

•

Sweetheart Strawberry Mousse

BLUSHING PINK ON TENDER GREENS

Once upon a time, supermarket produce sections displayed only two or three types of lettuce—iceberg, romaine, and perhaps butter. Now they offer an impressive array of fresh greens (see Glossary of Greens, p. 148).

1 cup butter or Boston lettuce
1 cup red leaf lettuce
1 cup spinach leaves, washed (no stems)
1 cup watercress leaves, packed (no stems)
1 cup mushrooms, thinly sliced
2 pink grapefruit, peeled and sectioned

Grapefruit Vinaigrette:
½ teaspoon garlic, minced
1 teaspoon Dijon mustard (optional)
2 tablespoons chives, snipped
¼ teaspoon dried basil leaves
¼ teaspoon dried oregano leaves
1 tablespoon olive oil
¼ cup fresh grapefruit juice

Tear greens into bite-size pieces; gently toss greens with mushrooms and grapefruit sections. Chill.

For the dressing: Combine garlic, mustard, chives, basil, oregano, olive oil, and grapefruit juice in a blender; process until thoroughly mixed. Chill.

When ready to serve, drizzle dressing over greens.

Serves 6

Per serving: 68 calories, 2 grams protein, 11 grams carbohydrate, 3 grams fat (32%), 0 milligrams cholesterol, 17 milligrams sodium.

BROCCOLI & CHEESE QUICHE

Slices of potato create a decorative (and nutritious) crust for this delicious entree. Dot with cream cheese chunks for a flavor sensation. "Loves and Quiches" for your sweetheart!

2 medium potatoes, thinly sliced
1 (10-ounce) package frozen chopped broccoli, thawed
⅔ cup green onion (white and green parts), sliced
1 (2-ounce) jar sliced pimento
4 egg whites
1 egg
⅓ cup plain low-fat yogurt
¼ cup low-fat milk
½ teaspoon dried basil leaves, crushed
⅛ teaspoon garlic powder
½ cup mozzarella cheese, grated
¼ cup Parmesan cheese, grated, divided
2 ounces reduced-calorie cream cheese
garnish: fresh basil

In a skillet sprayed with vegetable cooking spray, cook potatoes, covered, over medium-low heat until tender (about 10 to 15 minutes); turn occasionally. Remove from heat.

Arrange potato slices over bottom and around sides of a 9-inch quiche dish sprayed with vegetable cooking spray. Overlap the potatoes to form a decorative edge; set aside.

In a medium microwave-safe bowl, microwave broccoli and onion on HIGH for 2 minutes or until tender. Drain well. Arrange in the crust.

Reserve 1 pimento strip from jar. Drain and chop remaining pimentos. In a medium bowl, combine egg whites, egg, yogurt, milk, basil, garlic powder, pimento, mozzarella cheese, and 2 tablespoons Parmesan cheese. Turn into prepared dish. Sprinkle with remaining Parmesan cheese. Drop chunks of cream cheese over quiche. Cover potato crust with foil. Bake in a 375 degree oven for 10 minutes. Remove foil; bake about 15 minutes more or until knife inserted near center comes out clean. Let stand 10 minutes. Garnish with reserved pimento and fresh basil.

Serves 6

Per serving: 196 calories, 14 grams protein, 18 grams carbohydrate, 8 grams fat (36%), 67 milligrams cholesterol, 266 milligrams sodium.

Honey-Peach Bran Muffins

Besides tasting delicious, these muffins provide a nice fiber bonus. Substitute your choice of fruit and fruit yogurt for a versatile variation.

½ cup all-purpose flour
¾ cup whole-wheat flour
¼ cup wheat bran
1 teaspoon baking powder
1 teaspoon baking soda
1 teaspoon ground cinnamon
¼ cup honey
1 egg white, slightly beaten
1 (8-ounce) carton peach low-fat yogurt
¼ cup reduced-calorie margarine, melted
½ cup peaches canned in extra-light syrup, drained well and coarsely chopped

In a large bowl, combine flours, bran, baking powder, baking soda, and cinnamon.

In a small bowl, combine honey, egg white, yogurt, and margarine. Stir well. Add to dry ingredients. Stir until just moistened. Add peaches.

Spoon batter into muffin cups sprayed with vegetable cooking spray, filling ¾ full. Bake at 350 degrees for 18 to 20 minutes or until lightly browned.

Makes 12 muffins
Per serving: 114 calories, 3 grams protein, 21 grams carbohydrate, 3 grams fat (21%), 1 milligram cholesterol, 143 milligrams sodium.

Sweetheart Strawberry Mousse

An old Indian legend describes the strawberry as the fruit of love. No wonder my sweetheart becomes just a bit more amorous when this dessert is around!

2 pints fresh strawberries
2 envelopes unflavored gelatin
1 cup water
1 cup sugar
  juice of 1 lemon
1 teaspoon vanilla extract
1 cup nondairy whipped topping
2 egg whites
garnish: fresh strawberry fans*

Wash strawberries. Blot on paper towels. Hull and purée in blender.

Add gelatin to cold water in saucepan. Stir constantly over low heat until dissolved (about 5 minutes). Remove from heat and stir in sugar.

Combine mixture with berries. Add lemon juice and vanilla. Chill in freezer or refrigerator until mixture forms a ball when dropped from a spoon.

Whip egg whites until stiff peaks form. Fold egg whites into whipped topping. Fold berry mixture into egg white mixture. Transfer into dessert glasses or mold. Chill until set (at least 2 hours). Garnish with fresh strawberry fans.*

Serves 6
Per serving: 212 calories, 4 grams protein, 43 grams carbohydrate, 4 grams fat (14%), 0 milligrams cholesterol, 24 milligrams sodium.

*Place strawberry, hull down, on a board; make cuts in the berry, taking care not to slice all the way through. Make 4 cuts for small berries and 8 cuts for larger ones. Hold the strawberry gently and twist in the opposite direction so that the slices fan out. Carefully cut out the green hull with the point of a knife. Replace the hull with a sprig of fresh mint.

New Beginnings

Spring is a time for beginnings—fresh starts, if you will. New blades of green grass, births of babes, hands joined in marriage. Open the windows of your home, your heart, and your mind to feel refreshed by cool spring breezes.

M·E·N·U

*Spring Garden
Vegetable Soup*

•

*Medley of Baby Greens
&
Orange-Raspberry
Vinaigrette*

•

*Tender Spinach Crepes
&
Fresh
Basil-Tomato Sauce*

•

*Fresh Fruit Nestled in
Barley Salad*

•

*Layered Lemon Angel
Dessert
&
Strawberry Sauce*

Spring Garden Vegetable Soup

This soup makes a wonderful beginning to a spring meal. Tender young vegetables create a garden-fresh flavor. I think you'll find the herbs and spices are pleasant substitutes for salt.

2   tablespoons reduced-calorie margarine
6   cloves garlic, minced
1   cup green onions (white and green parts), sliced
2   (28-ounce) cans whole tomatoes, coarsely chopped
3   cups Vegetable Broth (see p. 91)
2   teaspoons dried tarragon leaves
2   teaspoons dried basil leaves
1   teaspoon dill weed
1   cup evaporated low-fat milk
4   small red new potatoes, diced
8   baby carrots, sliced
1   cup petite peas
1   cup fresh asparagus tips, each 2 inches long

Melt margarine in a large stockpot over low heat. Sauté the garlic and onions until onions are translucent. Add the tomatoes, broth, tarragon, basil, and dill weed. Add salt and pepper, if desired, to taste. Cover; simmer 30 minutes.

Purée the tomato mixture in a blender or food processor. Return the purée to the pot; stir in the evaporated milk.

Place potatoes and carrots in a medium microwave-safe bowl; microwave on HIGH for 7 to 8 minutes until vegetables are just tender. Set aside.

Just before serving, heat the soup over low heat. Add the reserved potatoes and carrots, the petite peas and asparagus tips. Cook for 5 minutes or until heated through. Serve immediately while the vegetables are tender.

Serves 10

Per 1 ½ cup serving: 138 calories, 7 grams protein, 22 grams carbohydrate, 3 grams fat (20%), 1 milligram cholesterol, 420 milligrams sodium.

❧
MEDLEY OF BABY GREENS & ORANGE-RASPBERRY VINAIGRETTE

Handle the greens carefully. Wash, dry, and wrap them in paper towels; then put them in a plastic bag and refrigerate for up to several days (see Glossary of Greens, p. 148).

6 cups (about 1 ½ pounds) greens (choose from butter or Boston, red or green leaf, oakleaf, mâche or lamb's lettuce, nasturtium, whatever is available), washed, stemmed, and drained

Orange-Raspberry Vinaigrette:
2 tablespoons orange juice
1 teaspoon raspberry preserves
3 tablespoons light olive oil
❧ *garnish:* edible flowers (such as nasturtiums or violets).*

Rinse and dry the greens well. Tear into bite-size pieces. Combine the greens in a large bowl. Cover and refrigerate for 30 to 45 minutes to keep crisp.

For the vinaigrette: Mix the orange juice and raspberry preserves in a small bowl. Slowly add the oil, whisking constantly until smooth. Season with salt and pepper, if desired, to taste.

When ready to serve, lightly toss the greens with vinaigrette and garnish with the edible flowers. Serve immediately.

Serves 8
Per serving: 54 calories, 1 gram protein, 9 grams carbohydrate, 2 grams fat (29%), 0 milligrams cholesterol, 5 milligrams sodium.

*Not only do flowers and herbs serve as garnishes and visual feasts, but they can please the palate as well. Please be careful. All flowers used for food must be grown in pesticide-free environments. Do not use commercially grown flowers for cooking. Consider nasturtium, rosemary, calendula, impatiens, rose, daisy, violet, pansy, rose geranium, arugula, viola, and borage.

Tender Spinach Crepes & Fresh Basil-Tomato Sauce

Making crepes takes practice, but once you learn to make them, you'll want to explore new ways of filling them. Crepes can be made ahead and refrigerated until ready for use. Store between layers of wax paper and wrap well. Reheat in a conventional or microwave oven.

Sauce:
- 12 large ripe Roma tomatoes, cored and cut into chunks, or 1 (28-ounce) can pear-shaped tomatoes
- 1 cup fresh basil, chopped, or 2 tablespoons dried basil leaves

Filling:
- 2 cups part-skim ricotta cheese
- 2 egg whites
- 1 pound spinach, stems trimmed and leaves shredded, cooked until tender, or 1 (10-ounce) package frozen chopped spinach, thawed and drained well
- 1 tablespoon Italian herb blend

Crepes:
- ½ cup all-purpose flour
- 1 egg
- 3 egg whites
- 1 cup low-fat milk
- *garnish:* ½ cup Parmesan cheese, grated

For the sauce: Purée tomatoes in a blender or food processor. Transfer tomatoes to a saucepan and add basil. Boil gently, uncovered, until sauce is reduced to 2 cups (30 to 50 minutes). As sauce thickens, lower heat and stir often.

For the filling: In a medium bowl, combine ricotta and egg whites; add ¼ teaspoon salt and pepper, if desired, or to taste. Add spinach and Italian herbs. Mix well.

For the crepes: Combine flour, egg, egg whites, and milk in a blender or food processor; process 30 seconds. Scrape sides with rubber spatula and blend another 30 seconds. Refrigerate 1 hour. When ready to make crepes, coat skillet with cooking spray; cook over medium heat. Pour 2 tablespoons batter in pan, tilting pan quickly in all directions to coat pan. Cook 1 minute or until lightly brown. Flip crepe and cook other side. Place crepes on towel to cool. Stack crepes between layers of wax paper.

Spoon an equal portion of spinach filling down center of each crepe; roll to enclose. Place single layer of crepes in a 10-inch pie or quiche dish sprayed with vegetable cooking spray. Spoon tomato sauce over crepes and sprinkle with Parmesan cheese.

Bake, uncovered, in a 375 degree oven until hot in center (30 to 40 minutes).

Serves 8
Per serving: 201 calories, 16 grams protein, 20 grams carbohydrate, 7 grams fat (31%), 24 milligrams cholesterol, 272 milligrams sodium.

Fresh Fruit Nestled in Barley Salad

Tangy citrus flavor makes this a refreshing salad all year long. Experiment with other grains you might have on hand, such as rice, couscous, or bulgur wheat. In the summer, add melons.

- 3 cups cooked barley
- 1 medium red apple, diced
- 1 medium green apple, diced
- 2 cups fresh strawberries, halved
- 1 medium banana, sliced
- 1 cup seedless grapes, halved
- 1 small cantaloupe, cut into chunks (if available)
- ¼ cup reduced-calorie maple syrup
- ¼ cup fresh lemon juice
- *garnish:* brown sugar or fruit-flavored low-fat yogurt

In a large bowl, combine barley and fruit. Combine maple syrup and lemon juice; add to barley-fruit mixture and toss gently. Cover and chill several hours or overnight. Garnish with sprinkle of brown sugar or dollop of yogurt.

Serves 8
Per 1 cup serving: 231 calories, 4 grams protein, 55 grams carbohydrate, 1 gram fat (3%), 0 milligrams cholesterol, 7 milligrams sodium.

LAYERED LEMON ANGEL DESSERT & STRAWBERRY SAUCE

I think, therefore I am.
—RENÉ DESCARTES

I was introduced to genuine English trifle while studying in London. Of course, the traditional trifle is full of rich pudding, cream, and cake. This luscious version is lower in calories and fat, but is equally as pleasing.

1 (4-serving size) box sugar-free instant lemon pudding and pie filling
2 cups cold low-fat milk
1 cup lemon low-fat yogurt
4 ounces reduced-calorie cream cheese rind of 1 lemon, finely grated
1 large angel food cake, cut in bite-size chunks
1 ½ cups fresh strawberries, sliced

Strawberry Sauce:
½ cup fresh strawberries, sliced
1 tablespoon apple juice or white grape juice
garnish: lemon slices and fresh mint leaves

In a food processor or electric blender, combine the pudding, low-fat milk, yogurt, cream cheese, and lemon rind. Blend until smooth.

For the sauce: Place strawberries and apple juice in a food processor or electric blender. Process until smooth. Chill.

When ready to serve, spread ⅓ of angel food cake chunks on bottom of a deep glass bowl or trifle dish; then layer with ⅓ of pudding mixture, then ½ of sliced strawberries; repeat, ending with pudding mixture. Spoon strawberry sauce over top. Garnish with lemon slices and fresh mint leaves.

Serves 12
Per serving: 203 calories, 7 grams protein, 38 grams carbohydrate, 3 grams fat (15%), 11 milligrams cholesterol, 371 milligrams sodium.

RAINY DAYS

Bright sunlight and wet, misty days signal spring's arrival; dormant winter life emerges and breathes the fresh air. We, too, shed winter coats. Spring, however, is full of surprises; always remember to plan for the "Rainy Day."

UNFORGETTABLE BAKED BEANS

Bring the picnic indoors on a rainy day and serve this delicious recipe that is certain to please. The pineapple and peppers create an unexpected flavor sensation.

1	pound dried navy or Great Northern beans
1	cup onion, chopped
2	cloves garlic, minced
¼	cup reduced-calorie margarine
½	cup brown sugar
1	cup catsup
6	tablespoons maple syrup
¼	cup light molasses
1	(14 ½-ounce) can peeled tomatoes
1	(20-ounce) can unsweetened pineapple tidbits, drained
2	cups (about 2 medium) green peppers, diced
2	tablespoons Worcestershire sauce

Rinse the beans. Soak them overnight in a large pot of water.

Rinse the soaked beans well under cold water; place them in a large saucepan. Cover with water and bring to a boil. Reduce the heat and simmer until tender (about 45 minutes to 1 hour). Drain, reserving ¾ cup cooking liquid.

In a 2-quart casserole dish or Dutch oven, over medium heat, sauté the onion and garlic in melted margarine until onions are translucent (about 5 minutes). Add the brown sugar and stir over medium-low heat until it has dissolved (about 5 minutes). Then stir in the catsup and the remaining ingredients. Add salt and pepper, if desired, to taste. Add the drained beans and mix well.

Cover the Dutch oven and transfer it to the oven. Bake in a preheated 300 degree oven, stirring occasionally, for 2 ½ hours.

Add the reserved bean liquid. Cover; bake 30 minutes. Then remove the cover and bake until the sauce is thick and syrupy (another 10 to 15 minutes). Serve hot.

Serves 10
Per 1 cup serving: 222 calories, 4 grams protein, 47 grams carbohydrate, 3 grams fat (13%), 0 milligrams cholesterol, 545 milligrams sodium.

M·E·N·U

*Unforgettable
Baked Beans*

•

Rustic Corn Bread

•

*Creamy
Spinach Dip
&
Fresh Vegetables*

•

Tropical Fruit Pasta

•

*Chewy Mint-Fudge
Brownies*

RUSTIC CORN BREAD

Picture yourself in the Old West—no electric blenders or food processors. This hearty bread only requires bowls, spoons, a pan, and an oven. It is real corn bread and matches the robust flavor of the baked beans.

1 cup stone-ground yellow cornmeal
¾ cup all-purpose flour
¼ cup whole-wheat flour
1 teaspoon baking powder
¼ teaspoon salt
½ teaspoon baking soda
1 cup canned cream-style corn
½ cup fresh or frozen corn kernels, thawed if frozen
½ cup plain low-fat yogurt
½ cup low-fat milk
1 egg, slightly beaten
2 egg whites, slightly beaten
2 tablespoons vegetable oil
¼ cup brown sugar, packed

Preheat the oven to 400 degrees. Spray an 8-inch square baking pan with vegetable cooking spray.

In a large mixing bowl, combine the cornmeal, flours, baking powder, salt, and baking soda.

In a medium bowl, combine the remaining ingredients; stir until smooth. Add half the liquid mixture to the dry mixture, stirring just until blended. Add the remaining liquid and again stir just until blended. Transfer the batter to the prepared pan.

Bake until the top is golden and a knife inserted in the center comes out clean (about 25 minutes). Cool slightly in the pan before cutting into squares.

Serves 8

Per serving: 192 calories, 5 grams protein, 24 grams carbohydrate, 4 grams fat (19%), 29 milligrams cholesterol, 236 milligrams sodium.

CREAMY SPINACH DIP & FRESH VEGETABLES

When fruit and vegetable prices start to decrease at the supermarket, we know that spring is right around the corner. Create your own combinations of vegetables; just be sure to have plenty of this flavorful dip on hand.

1 ½ cups low-fat cottage cheese
½ cup reduced-calorie mayonnaise
2 tablespoons fresh lemon juice
1 teaspoon sugar
½ teaspoon salt
½ teaspoon paprika
½ teaspoon garlic powder
¼ teaspoon onion powder
¼ teaspoon celery seeds
¼ teaspoon Italian herb blend
2 cups fresh spinach, finely chopped, or 1 (10-ounce) package frozen chopped spinach, thawed and drained
1 (8-ounce) can water chestnuts, drained and sliced
cherry tomatoes, snow peas, carrot sticks, cauliflower florets, and green pepper slices

In a food processor or blender, process cottage cheese, mayonnaise, lemon juice, sugar, salt, paprika, garlic and onion powders, celery seeds, and Italian herb blend until smooth. Add pepper, if desired, to taste. Transfer mixture to bowl. Add spinach and water chestnuts; stir well. Cover and refrigerate at least 4 hours to blend flavors. Then stir and serve with fresh vegetables.

Makes about 1 ⅓ cups

Per 1 cup vegetables and 2 tablespoons dip: 127 calories, 8 grams protein, 14 grams carbohydrate, 5 grams fat (36%), 6 milligrams cholesterol, 322 milligrams sodium.

Let the rain kiss you. Let the rain beat upon your head with silver liquid drops.
—LANGSTON HUGHES

❧ TROPICAL FRUIT PASTA

Rain's a mixed-up sort of weather,
Pro and con all rolled up together.
—RICHARD ARMOUR

Rainy days are great for daydreaming. Now picture yourself on a resort island, soaking up the tropical sun while enjoying this refreshing pasta dish. It is packed full of the sunny island's best flavors. Aloha!

½ cup sugar
1 tablespoon flour
1 cup unsweetened pineapple juice
1 egg white, slightly beaten
2 tablespoons lemon juice
1 ½ quarts water
8 ounces small round pasta
1 (11-ounce) can mandarin oranges
1 (20-ounce) can pineapple tidbits, drained
½ cup nondairy whipped topping
6 ounces piña colada low-fat yogurt
❧ *garnish:* banana slices

In a small saucepan, combine sugar and flour. Gradually add pineapple juice and egg white. Cook over moderate heat, stirring until thickened. Add lemon juice. Cool to room temperature.

Cook pasta in boiling water according to package directions. Drain and rinse; cool to room temperature.

Combine pineapple juice mixture and pasta. Mix lightly but thoroughly. Refrigerate overnight.

Add mandarin oranges and pineapple tidbits; combine whipped topping and yogurt. Add to chilled pineapple mixture. Mix lightly but thoroughly. Chill.

When ready to serve, garnish with banana slices.

Serves 12
Per ¾ cup serving: 168 calories, 3 grams protein, 39 grams carbohydrate, 1 gram fat (6%), less than 1 milligram cholesterol, 16 milligrams sodium.

❧ CHEWY MINT-FUDGE BROWNIES

If you love chewy chocolate, you will adore these treats just as much as my family does. Serve alone or dress up the brownies with vanilla ice milk and chocolate sauce.

¾ cup sugar
¼ cup reduced-calorie margarine, softened
2 tablespoons water
2 teaspoons vanilla extract
2 egg whites, divided, at room temperature
¾ cup all-purpose flour
⅓ cup unsweetened cocoa
¼ teaspoon baking powder
8 starlight candies, finely crushed

Beat sugar and margarine at medium speed of an electric mixer until crumbly. Add water, vanilla, and 1 egg white; on low speed, beat until well blended.

Combine flour, cocoa, baking powder, and crushed candies; add to sugar mixture, stirring just until moistened. Set aside.

Beat remaining egg white in a small bowl at high speed until stiff peaks form; gently fold into flour mixture. Pour batter into an 8-inch-square baking pan coated with vegetable cooking spray. Bake at 350 degrees for about 25 minutes or until a wooden pick inserted in center comes out clean. Cool in pan on a wire rack.

Makes 12 squares
Per serving: 129 calories, 2 grams protein, 24 grams carbohydrate, 3 grams fat (22%), 0 milligrams cholesterol, 5 milligrams sodium.

BLOOMS OF THE SEASON

♣
SPRING-GREEN TORTELLINI SALAD

Days are getting longer and warmer. Spring arrives with the first show of new blooms, while tender leaves and stems beg to greet the sun. The emerging colors of spring inspired this light pasta recipe. For a variation, substitute Marinara Sauce (see p. 85) for the oil dressing.

¼ cup Vegetable Broth (see p. 91)
2 cloves garlic, minced
3-4 green onions (white and green parts), sliced
4 ounces fresh shiitake mushrooms, stems removed, caps sliced*
2 medium carrots, pared, cut into 1-inch julienne strips
1 cup snow peas, strings removed
1 (4.4-ounce) jar marinated artichoke hearts, drained and slivered, with marinade reserved
⅓ cup black olives, pitted and sliced
3 tablespoons fresh lemon juice
1 teaspoon Dijon mustard (optional)
2 tablespoons Parmesan cheese, grated
1 (16-ounce) package cheese-filled spinach tortellini
¼ cup fresh parsley, chopped, or 1 tablespoon dried parsley

Heat broth in a large skillet over medium heat. Add garlic, green onions, mushrooms, and carrots; cook, stirring occasionally, until vegetables are crisp-tender. Add peas and cook 2 minutes longer. Transfer vegetables to large pasta bowl. Add artichoke hearts and olives; toss to combine.

For the dressing: Whisk lemon juice, reserved artichoke marinade, mustard, and Parmesan cheese in small bowl until blended.

Cook and drain tortellini according to package directions. Add pasta to vegetables. Pour dressing over mixture and toss well. Season with salt and pepper, if desired, to taste. Sprinkle with parsley. Serve warm or cold.

Serves 8

Per serving: 196 calories, 9 grams protein, 24 grams carbohydrate, 8 grams fat (36%), 11 milligrams cholesterol, 351 milligrams sodium.

*Choose from a wide variety of spring mushrooms. White Domestic: Nicknamed button, this widely available mushroom is bland, but absorbs flavors well when added to dishes.

Shiitake: This versatile, aromatic mushroom has an earthy flavor and plump flesh. It's ideal for stuffing or adding to stir-fries.

Porcini: Also known as cèpe, this full-flavored European import is hearty enough to serve as a main course. It usually is sold dried.

Oyster Mushroom: This mushroom is tender fleshed, delicately flavored, and delicious in soups and light sauces.

Enoki: This tiny white-capped variety has very long sprout-like stems. Its fruity flavor is best enjoyed raw in salads or sandwiches, stir-fried, or sautéed gently.

M·E·N·U

Spring-Green Tortellini Salad

•

Fresh Asparagus Bundles & Crunchy Apricot Topping

•

Bagel Crisps

•

Honey-Lime Mango

•

Tropical Strawberry Sherbet

❧ Fresh Asparagus Bundles & Crunchy Apricot Topping

Buttercups and daisies,
Oh, the pretty flowers;
Coming ere
the Springtime.
—MARY HOWITT

Bright emerald asparagus spears herald the promise of spring. Treat them tenderly. Enjoy asparagus as quickly as you can because age destroys its natural vitamins A and C.

2 pounds fresh asparagus
5-6 green onions (green stems only)
2 teaspoons reduced-calorie margarine
3 tablespoons almonds, coarsely chopped
½ cup low-sugar apricot spread

Snap off tough ends of asparagus. Arrange asparagus in a microwave-safe dish; microwave on HIGH for 3 to 4 minutes until crisp-tender. Tie green onion stems around 3 or 4 asparagus spears to make a bundle; repeat, making 8 bundles. Arrange on a serving platter and keep warm.

For the topping: Melt margarine in a small saucepan over low heat; sauté almonds until lightly toasted. Stir in apricot spread; cook until heated. Spoon over asparagus bundles.

Serves 8
Per serving: 77 calories, 4 grams protein, 11 grams carbohydrate, 3 grams fat (31%), 0 milligrams cholesterol, 17 milligrams sodium.

❧ Bagel Crisps

Bagels are so very versatile. Top them with fruit, peanut butter, cream cheese, pizza sauce. In this recipe, I turned them into modified croutons with less fat than most croutons.

3 tablespoons reduced-calorie margarine
1 ½ teaspoons dried oregano leaves
¾ teaspoon garlic powder
4 bagels, cut ¼ inch thick, approximately 4 slices per bagel

Combine margarine, oregano, and garlic powder; divide evenly and spread on each bagel slice.

Place bagel slices, spread side up, on a baking sheet; broil 6 inches from heat for 1 minute or until golden.

Makes about 16
Per 2 slices: 137 calories, 4 grams protein, 17 grams carbohydrate, 6 grams fat (37%), 0 milligrams cholesterol, 167 milligrams sodium.

❧ Honey-Lime Mango

Add the goodness of honey and the spark of lime to ripe mangos and create an unforgettable taste sensation.

3 large ripe mangos
juice of 3 limes
3 tablespoons honey

Peel mangos. Cut flesh off pit into long slices; place on serving plate.

In a small bowl, mix lime juice and honey; drizzle over mangos. Serve immediately or refrigerate, covered. Serve cold with Tropical Strawberry Sherbet.

Serves 6
Per serving: 88 calories, less than 1 gram protein, 23 grams carbohydrate, less than 1 gram fat (2%), 0 milligrams cholesterol, 2 milligrams sodium.

✍

TROPICAL STRAWBERRY SHERBET

The first fruits of the season combine beautifully in this luscious frozen dessert. Refreshing, colorful!

2   cups fresh strawberries, halved
2   cups (about 3 medium) ripe bananas, sliced
¼   cup sugar
1   (6-ounce) can frozen pineapple juice concentrate, thawed and undiluted
¼   teaspoon almond extract
½   cup plain low-fat yogurt
🌿   *garnish:* fresh mint leaves

Place strawberries, bananas, sugar, pineapple juice concentrate, and almond extract in a food processor or electric blender; process until smooth. Transfer mixture to a medium bowl; add yogurt, stirring well.

Pour mixture into freezer container of a 1-gallon ice cream freezer (hand turned or electric). Follow manufacturer's instructions to freeze the mixture.

Makes 10 servings

Per ½ cup serving: 96 calories, 1 gram protein, 23 grams carbohydrate, less than 1 gram fat (4%), less than 1 milligram cholesterol, 9 milligrams sodium.

*Each opening sweet of earliest bloom,
And rifle all
the breathing spring.*
—WILLIAM COLLINS

KITES AND KITTENS

Mealtimes should be pleasant experiences—not battlegrounds. You decide what is to be served; then allow your child to choose what, if any, foods to eat. Trust in the child's ability to regulate his or her own intake. (Remember, your child did this as an infant.) Let the youngster choose from a wide variety of foods. Use colors and shapes creatively. Encourage your child to assist you in the preparations.

♣

ENCHANTED FOREST PASTA & HERB DRESSING

A little creativity goes a long way when it comes to getting children to try new dishes. Create an imaginary forest by using the various vegetables and pasta for colorful trees, shrubs, and plants.

 1 cup fresh broccoli florets
 1 cup fresh carrots, sliced
 1 cup fresh zucchini, sliced
12 ounces rotini noodles, rainbow mix
½ cup red onion, chopped
 2 cloves garlic, minced
 1 tablespoon reduced-calorie margarine
 1 cup green pepper, cut into ½-inch strips
½ cup mushrooms, sliced
🌼 *garnish:* tomato and fresh parsley

Herb Dressing:
¼ cup lemon juice
 1 teaspoon sugar
 2 tablespoons Parmesan cheese, grated
 2 tablespoons fresh basil, minced, or 2 teaspoons dried basil leaves
 2 tablespoons olive oil
 1 clove garlic, minced

Steam or microwave broccoli, carrots, and zucchini until crisp-tender (about 6 or 7 minutes).

Cook rotini according to package directions until tender.

Sauté onion and garlic in melted margarine until onions are translucent. Add green pepper and mushrooms; cook for 1 minute. Add ¼ teaspoon salt and pepper, if desired, or to taste.

For the dressing: Combine all ingredients in mixing bowl; stir well.

Place noodles in pasta dish; top with steamed vegetables, onion mixture, and dressing. Toss gently. Garnish with chopped tomato and snipped parsley.

Serves 8
Per serving: 134 calories, 4 grams protein, 19 grams carbohydrate, 5 grams fat (33%), 1 milligram cholesterol, 41 milligrams sodium.

M·E·N·U

Enchanted Forest Pasta
&
Herb Dressing
•
Egg Salad Sandwiches

Fresh Fruit Kabobs
&
Creamy Cherry Dip
•
Baked Apple Cages

Pinwheels & Pencils

EGG SALAD SANDWICHES

An egg is a complete protein containing all nine essential amino acids, the protein building blocks. It also has generous amounts of vitamin A and iron. And children will eat eggs when practically everything else fails. Vary the toppings of this delicious sandwich to suit your youngster's preferences.

  4 hard-cooked eggs, peeled and chopped (remove 1 egg yolk)
  ¼ cup cucumber, unpeeled and finely diced
3-4 green onions (white and green parts), sliced
  ¼ cup celery, chopped
  1 tablespoon reduced-calorie mayonnaise
  1 tablespoon plain low-fat yogurt
  ¼ teaspoon dried dill weed
  ¼ teaspoon celery seed
  4 whole-grain deli rolls
  1 cup alfalfa sprouts, divided
  4 lettuce leaves
  4 tomato slices

Combine eggs, cucumber, green onions, and celery in a bowl; toss gently and set aside.

In a small bowl, stir together mayonnaise, yogurt, dill weed, and celery seed. Add salt and pepper, if desired, to taste; add to egg mixture, stirring well. Cover and chill.

Spread about ¼ of the egg mixture on half of each bun and top with ¼ cup alfalfa sprouts. Line the other half of each bun with a lettuce leaf and tomato slice.

Makes 4 sandwiches
Per serving: 232 calories, 9 grams protein, 31 grams carbohydrate, 8 grams fat (30%), 157 milligrams cholesterol, 397 milligrams sodium.

FRESH FRUIT KABOBS & CREAMY CHERRY DIP

When children participate in meal preparations, they are more likely to eat. These easy kabobs on popsicle sticks let kids experiment with color combinations for lots of learning fun.

  1 cup fresh pineapple, cut into chunks
  2 medium apples, unpeeled and cut into 1-inch chunks
  2 small bananas, sliced 1 inch thick
 16 seedless green grapes
  8 fresh strawberries, halved
     orange juice, unsweetened

Creamy Cherry Dip:
  ½ cup reduced-calorie cream cheese
  ½ cup cherry low-fat yogurt
  ¼ cup marshmallow creme

Thread fruit onto 16 popsicle sticks. Brush with orange juice.

For the dip: In a medium mixing bowl, combine all ingredients. Beat on low until well blended. Cover and chill 2 hours. Serve with kabobs.

Makes 16
Per kabob: 78 calories, 1 gram protein, 15 grams carbohydrate, 2 grams fat (22%), 6 milligrams cholesterol, 36 milligrams sodium.

Don't go into Mr. McGregor's garden; your Father had an accident there; he was put in a pie by Mrs. McGregor.
—BEATRIX POTTER

♣

Baked Apple Cages

Purchased puff pastry is great for children. They can cut and shape it into whatever their imaginations can create. Then, decorate or flavor with cinnamon and sugar, sprinkles, or raisins and seeds; bake until golden brown. In this recipe, children can wrap the apples and sprinkle the sugar, and, of course, eat them.

4 small tart cooking apples (such as Jonathan or Winesap), peeled and cored
¼ cup raisins
¼ cup Granola, homemade or purchased (see p. 63)
2 tablespoons almonds, chopped
¼ cup brown sugar, packed
½ cup water
2 tablespoons reduced-calorie margarine, melted
1 teaspoon ground cinnamon
1 sheet frozen puff pastry, cut into 16 strips (½-inch wide) and 4 leaf shapes
1 egg, beaten
2 tablespoons sugar

Place apples in a 5-by-7-inch microwave-safe dish. Combine raisins, granola, and almonds. Fill apples with raisin mixture.

In a small bowl, combine brown sugar, water, margarine, and cinnamon; pour around apples.

Cover with wax paper. Microwave on HIGH for 6 to 8 minutes or just until tender. Remove apples and cool slightly. Keep brown sugar syrup warm.

Place 1 pastry strip around each apple, tucking in the ends underneath. Place another strip across the first strip and tuck underneath. Cross remaining 2 strips of pastry over the apple at even intervals and tuck securely. Place leaves or other cut shapes on each apple. Brush with beaten egg; sprinkle with 2 tablespoons sugar.

Place wrapped apples on a cookie sheet sprayed with vegetable cooking spray. Bake in a 400 degree oven for 15 minutes or until pastry is golden brown. Pour reserved syrup over apples and serve warm with vanilla ice milk, if desired.

Makes 4 apples
Per ½ apple: 160 calories, 1 gram protein, 27 grams carbohydrate, 6 grams fat (34%), 4 milligrams cholesterol, 51 milligrams sodium.

♣

Pinwheels & Pencils

Have fun with shapes and sizes as your children help you mix all the "yummy" ingredients in this recipe. Youngsters can add a few of their own favorite snack treats for a variation.

2 cups pinwheel-shaped honey graham snack crackers
2 cups small unsalted pretzels
2 cups bite-size whole-wheat crackers
2 cups crispy wheat, corn, or rice cereal squares
1 cup crispy oat-bran cereal squares
½ cup dry-roasted unsalted peanuts
¼ cup semisweet chocolate chip morsels (optional)

Combine all ingredients in a large bowl or store in a large zip-top plastic bag.

Makes about 10 cups
Per 1 cup: 192 calories, 5 grams protein, 28 grams carbohydrate, 8 grams fat (34%), 0 milligrams cholesterol, 213 milligrams sodium.

Mother's Lap

My mother is gifted with a unique sense of humor, an appreciation for lovely things, and an unparalleled zest for life. Many of my mother's favorite dishes inspired this simple brunch menu.

Want to do something especially memorable for Mother's Day this year? Prepare and serve a delicious brunch. This menu is chock-full of luscious and nutritious dishes that are simple to fix and that feature some of spring's choicest fruits and vegetables.

Omelet Primavera & Orange Sauce

Omelets are one of my mother's specialties. This recipe combines crisp vegetables with a blend of orange and basil in a puffy egg shell.

- 1 cup fresh asparagus tips
- 1 cup small broccoli florets
- ½ cup small red bell pepper, chopped
- ½ cup yellow squash, julienne-cut (2 inches long)
- 4 egg yolks
- 2 tablespoons unsweetened orange juice
- 1 teaspoon fresh basil, chopped, or ¼ teaspoon dried basil leaves
- 6 egg whites, at room temperature
- 1 tablespoon all-purpose flour

Orange Sauce:

- ½ cup unsweetened orange juice,
- 1 teaspoon cornstarch
- rind of 1 orange, cut into ¼-inch-wide strips
- 2 teaspoons sugar
- ½ teaspoon fresh basil, chopped, or pinch of dried basil leaves
- *garnish:* orange sections and fresh basil

Microwave asparagus, broccoli, bell pepper, and squash in a microwave-safe bowl on HIGH for 5 to 6 minutes until crisp-tender; set aside.

Beat egg yolks until thick. Add orange juice and basil. Blend well with a whisk, set aside.

Beat egg whites until soft peaks form. Add flour and continue beating until stiff peaks form. Fold into egg yolk mixture.

Pour ⅓ of egg mixture into a skillet sprayed with vegetable cooking spray, spreading evenly. Cook about 5 minutes, covered, or until center is firm. Arrange ⅓ of vegetable mixture over half of omelet. Use a spatula to loosen and fold omelet. Transfer omelet onto a plate. Repeat procedure for additional omelets.

For the sauce: Combine orange juice, cornstarch, orange rind, sugar, and basil in a small saucepan, stirring well; place over medium heat. Cook 3 minutes or until slightly thickened.

Cut each omelet in half. Serve with orange sauce; garnish with orange slices and basil.

Serves 6

Per serving: 110 calories, 8 grams protein, 12 grams carbohydrate, 4 grams fat (32%), 183 milligrams cholesterol, 67 milligrams sodium.

M·E·N·U

Omelet Primavera
&
Orange Sauce
•
Bran Muffins
With Blueberries
•
Seven-Grain Cereal
&
Fresh Fruit Medley
•
Citrus Banana
Wake-up

⁊ BRAN MUFFINS WITH BLUEBERRIES

Enjoy the high fiber goodness of these fruit-filled muffins. Although honey claims no specific nutrient advantage over other sugar forms, you probably will use less because honey is more concentrated.

1 ½ cups whole-bran cereal
  ¾ cup buttermilk
  ⅓ cup honey
  ¼ cup vegetable oil
  2 egg whites
  1 cup all-purpose flour
  ½ cup oat or wheat bran
2 ½ teaspoons baking powder
  ½ teaspoon baking soda
  ½ teaspoon salt
  1 cup blueberries

In a large bowl, combine bran cereal, buttermilk, honey, oil, and egg whites; let stand for 10 minutes.

In a second bowl, combine flour, oat or wheat bran, baking powder, baking soda, and salt; add to cereal mixture and stir until just moistened. Gently fold in blueberries. Spoon batter into muffin cups sprayed with vegetable cooking spray, filling ¾ full.

Bake for 25 minutes in a 400 degree oven or until a wooden pick comes out clean. Cool in pan for 5 minutes; remove from pan and cool completely on a wire rack.

Makes 9 muffins

Per muffin: 201 calories, 5 grams protein, 35 grams carbohydrate, 7 grams fat (28%), less than 1 milligram cholesterol, 386 milligrams sodium.

♣ SEVEN-GRAIN CEREAL & FRESH FRUIT MEDLEY

We once had to go to the local health-food store to locate some of the whole grains used in this cereal. Fortunately, supermarkets now stock their shelves with these hearty grains (see Grazing on Grains, p. 147). Keep this mix on hand, scooping out a cup or two to serve hot for a breakfast cereal or to cook and chill for a salad. Warm fresh fruit adds a nice touch.

1 ½ cups oat groats (uncut oats)
1 ½ cups long-grain brown rice
  1 cup whole-grain rye
1 ½ cups whole-grain whole wheat
  1 cup whole-grain buckwheat
  1 cup pearl barley
  1 cup millet
  1 cup whole sesame seeds (optional)

Fresh Fruit Medley:
  3 tablespoons unsweetened pineapple juice
  1 tablespoon honey
  ½ cup strawberries, halved
  ½ cup banana, sliced
  ½ cup tangerine, peeled and sectioned

Mix together oats, rice, rye, whole wheat, buckwheat, barley, and millet. (If desired, store up to 3 months in an airtight container in a cool, dry place.)

In a 2- to 3-quart pan on high heat, bring 2 ½ cups water or Vegetable Broth (see p. 91) to a boil. Add 1 cup grain mix. Cover, reduce heat; cook until grains are tender (about 25 minutes). Drain.

For the medley: Combine pineapple juice and honey in a saucepan; add strawberries, banana, and tangerine, stirring gently. Place over medium-low heat; cook 3 minutes or until warm. Spoon over cooked cereal. Variations: Top with milk, brown sugar, Three-Apple Topping (see p. 114), or Spiced Fruit Compote (see p. 103).

Serves 4

Per ½ cup cereal and 2 tablespoons medley: 194 calories, 5 grams protein, 38 grams carbohydrate, 3 grams fat (14%), 0 milligrams cholesterol, 4 milligrams sodium.

CITRUS-BANANA WAKE-UP

My mother created this tasty breakfast shake to ensure a healthful, delicious start to our day. Vary the fruit and yogurt flavors for a completely different taste experience.

2 tablespoons wheat germ
2 medium bananas, cut in 1-inch slices
1 cup unsweetened orange juice
1 cup vanilla low-fat yogurt
4 ice cubes

In a blender, process wheat germ until finely ground. Add banana, orange juice, yogurt, and ice cubes. Blend until smooth and pour into glasses.

Serves 4
Per 6 ounces: 146 calories, 4 grams protein, 32 grams carbohydrate, 1 gram fat (7%), 3 milligrams cholesterol, 34 milligrams sodium.

LEGACIES

Fads come and go; classics endure the test of time. This is true for fashion, automobiles, and food. Many ethnic dishes fall into the classic category: European, Middle Eastern, Asian, and American. A common thread of ethnic origin ties the recipes in this menu together. Invite guests to wear attire from the past and come prepared to share a bit of personal history.

♣

ITALIAN STUFFED ARTICHOKES

Artichokes are a good source of vitamins A and C, calcium, iron, and potassium. Choose large artichokes for this recipe and pick the roundest artichokes because they have the largest hearts. Rub any cut you make with lemon juice to avoid discoloration. This dish is a great start to a flavorful menu.

 2 large artichokes
 ½ lemon
 ¾ cup (about 2 medium) yellow squash, finely chopped
 ¼ cup seasoned bread crumbs
 2 tablespoons Parmesan cheese, grated
 ¼ cup part-skim mozzarella cheese, grated
 1 tablespoon reduced-calorie margarine, melted
 1 teaspoon dried oregano leaves
 1 teaspoon dried parsley
 ½ teaspoon dried basil leaves
 1 clove garlic, minced
 ❧ *garnish:* fresh parsley sprigs

Cut stems and 1 inch off the top of the artichokes. Rub cuts with lemon. Place artichokes upright in a microwave-safe plate. Add ½ cup water; cover with plastic wrap and microwave on HIGH for 12 minutes or until the stem end feels tender when pierced with a fork. Let stand 5 minutes. Drain, reserving liquid.

In a medium bowl, combine the squash, bread crumbs, Parmesan cheese, mozzarella cheese, margarine, oregano, parsley, basil, garlic, and reserved liquid. Add ¼ teaspoon salt and pepper, if desired, or to taste.

Cut each artichoke in half lengthwise. Using a serrated spoon, cut out the fuzzy choke and the small leaves in the center. Spoon vegetable mixture into the cavity. Cover loosely with plastic wrap. Microwave on HIGH for 3 minutes. Garnish with fresh parsley sprigs and serve.

Serves 4

Per serving: 135 calories, 8 grams protein, 15 grams carbohydrate, 5 grams fat (35%), 10 milligrams cholesterol, 257 milligrams sodium.

M·E·N·U

Italian Stuffed Artichokes

•

Vegetable & Tofu Stir-Fry

•

Carrot, Raisin, & Orange Salad

•

Fruit Salad & Creamy Yogurt Topping

•

Bananas Foster

♣

VEGETABLE & TOFU STIR-FRY

Asian cooking techniques are very simple: Keep it fresh, with little cooking time. Stir-fry is gaining greater acceptance in this country as we reduce fat and increase the fresh vegetables and whole grains in our meals.

Marinade:

1	small onion, finely chopped
¼	cup peanut oil
¼	cup lemon juice
¼	cup reduced-sodium soy sauce
2	teaspoons honey
1	tablespoon fresh ginger, grated
2	cloves garlic, minced or crushed

8	ounces firm tofu (in one-inch chunks)
1	tablespoon vegetable oil
1	teaspoon fresh ginger, grated
2	cloves garlic, minced
1	cup mung bean sprouts
5-6	green onions (white and green parts), sliced
1	cup (1 medium) red bell pepper, diced
1	cup mushrooms, sliced
2	cups Chinese cabbage, shredded
6	cups cooked brown rice or 12 ounces Chinese noodles, cooked and drained

In a small bowl, combine the marinade ingredients. Add the tofu chunks. Refrigerate for several hours.

Drain the tofu. Reserve ½ cup of marinade. Strain it into a small saucepan. Warm the marinade over low heat.

In a wok or skillet, heat the oil until it begins to smoke (about 30 seconds). Add ginger and garlic; sauté over medium heat for 1 to 2 minutes. Increase the heat and add the tofu chunks. Stir-fry for 2 to 3 minutes until tofu starts browning.

Slide the tofu to one side of the wok or skillet. Add vegetables and stir constantly for 2 to 3 minutes or until vegetables are crisp-tender.

Add 2 tablespoons of the warmed marinade. Cook for another 3 minutes.

Serve over rice or Chinese noodles.

Serves 6
Per serving: 333 calories, 10 grams protein, 58 grams carbohydrate, 8 grams fat (20%), 0 milligrams cholesterol, 239 milligrams sodium.

♣

CARROT, RAISIN, & ORANGE SALAD

This salad is a combination of classic American and Mediterranean recipes. This version is sweet and spicy, not high in fat like its traditional counterparts.

1	pound (about 5) carrots, peeled and grated
1	cup raisins
2	oranges, peeled and sectioned
1	Granny Smith apple, peeled and chopped
1	teaspoon ground cinnamon
3	tablespoons fresh lemon juice
1	tablespoon fresh mint, chopped

In a large bowl, combine carrots, raisins, oranges, apple, cinnamon, and lemon juice. Add a pinch of salt, if desired. Refrigerate until ready to serve.

Just before serving, toss with the mint.

Serves 8
Per serving: 108 calories, 1 gram protein, 28 grams carbohydrate, less than 1 gram fat (2%), 0 milligrams cholesterol, 18 milligrams sodium.

Fruit Salad &
Creamy Yogurt Topping

The classic 24-hour fruit salad is updated with a healthful topping. Select from summer's best fruits for color, texture, and shape contrasts.

1 medium peach, pitted and sliced
1 medium nectarine, pitted and sliced
1 pint strawberries, hulled and halved
1 cup cantaloupe, cut into bite-size chunks or balls
1 cup honeydew melon, cut into bite-size chunks or balls
1 cup fresh pineapple, cut in chunks

Creamy Yogurt Topping:
1 (8-ounce) carton piña colada low-fat yogurt
1 cup nondairy whipped topping
2 tablespoons fresh lime juice
garnish: fresh mint sprigs

Combine the fruit; refrigerate until ready to serve.

For the Creamy Yogurt Topping: Mix together the yogurt, whipped topping, and lime juice until well blended. Chill.

When ready to serve, spoon topping over fruit.

Serves 12

Per serving: 72 calories, 1 gram protein, 13 grams carbohydrate, 2 grams fat (24%), 1 milligram cholesterol, 15 milligrams sodium.

Bananas Foster

I have altered my all-time personal favorite classic dessert into this flavorful, low-fat version. By using a microwave oven, I can serve it within 10 minutes.

¼ cup frozen unsweetened apple juice concentrate
¾ teaspoon artificial rum flavoring*
1 teaspoon vanilla extract
3 tablespoons brown sugar, packed
3 tablespoons reduced-calorie margarine, melted
4 bananas, peeled and sliced lengthwise, then quartered
½ teaspoon ground cinnamon
¼ teaspoon ground allspice
⅛ teaspoon ground nutmeg
dash of ground cloves
vanilla ice milk

In a small bowl, stir the apple juice, rum flavoring, and vanilla together. Set aside.

In a 1-quart microwave-safe dish, combine the brown sugar and the melted margarine. Place the banana quarters in the mixture, coating them well. Arrange the bananas, flat side down, in the dish. Sprinkle with cinnamon, allspice, nutmeg, and cloves; cover with plastic wrap and microwave on HIGH for 1 minute.

Drizzle the apple juice mixture over the bananas. Return to the microwave and cook on HIGH for 1 minute.

Place a scoop of ice milk in the center of each dessert plate and arrange bananas around it. Top with the warm sauce and serve immediately.

Serves 4

Per serving: 310 calories, 4 grams protein, 58 grams carbohydrate, 9 grams fat (24%), 9 milligrams cholesterol, 123 milligrams sodium.

*Alcohol-free rum flavoring may be purchased at nutrition and health-food stores.

MIDSUMMER NIGHT'S DREAM

Perhaps friends have gathered for a preconcert dinner on a comfortable summer evening. Keep the menu casual and light so that you can enjoy the performance. Save the dessert for an encore later.

♣

BERRY-PEACH SOUP

Steady hands are what this decorative soup takes to combine two soups into one. The blend of flavors is as impressive as the presentation.

Berry Soup:
- ¾ cup fresh orange juice
- 3 tablespoons fresh lemon or lime juice
- 2 tablespoons sugar
- ¼ teaspoon ground cinnamon
  dash of ground nutmeg
- 2 pints fresh berries (strawberries, raspberries, or blackberries), rinsed and drained

Peach Soup:
- ¾ cup fresh orange juice
- 3 tablespoons lemon juice
- 2 tablespoons sugar
- 4 cups fresh peaches, peeled and chopped

For the Berry Soup: Place all ingredients in container of food processor or electric blender. Process until smooth. If desired, pour into a strainer over a bowl; discard seeds. Cover and chill. Stir before using.

For the Peach Soup: Place all ingredients in container of food processor or electric blender. Process until smooth. Cover and chill. Stir before using.

When ready to serve, pour berry and peach soups into separate pitchers. Hold a pitcher in each hand. Pour soups, simultaneously and slowly, into a soup bowl. Repeat procedure with remaining bowls.

Serves 8

Per serving: 118 calories, 2 grams protein, 28 grams carbohydrate, less than 1 gram fat (0%), less than 1 milligram cholesterol, 8 milligrams sodium.

M·E·N·U

Berry-Peach Soup

•

*Summer Squash
Soufflé*

•

*Green Beans
With Blue Cheese &
Almonds*

•

*Whole-Wheat Potato
Bread*

•

Good Earth Salad

•

Blueberry Cheesecake

SUMMER SQUASH SOUFFLÉ

Think of this recipe when your neighbor offers you more squash from his garden.* Soufflés can be tricky, but are worth the effort.

- 4 cups (about 2 pounds) summer squash, (include zucchini, yellow crookneck, and pattypan), sliced
- 3 tablespoons reduced-calorie margarine, divided
- 1 medium onion, diced
- 1 cup (about ¼ pound) mushrooms, sliced
- ¼ cup Parmesan cheese, grated
- 1 cup part-skim ricotta cheese
- 1 cup low-fat cottage cheese
- 3 eggs, lightly beaten
- 4 egg whites
- ¼ cup cheddar cheese, grated
- ½ cup dry bread crumbs

Place summer squash in a microwave-safe dish; microwave on HIGH for 3 to 4 minutes or until crisp-tender. Drain excess liquid.

While the squash is cooking, melt 2 tablespoons margarine in a skillet. Add onion and sauté until translucent. Add the mushrooms and sauté until soft.

Add the sautéed vegetables and Parmesan cheese to the summer squash. Add salt and pepper, if desired, to taste.

In a food processor or electric blender, combine ricotta and cottage cheeses. Process until smooth. Add ricotta mixture and eggs to squash mixture. Combine thoroughly.

Beat the egg whites until stiff peaks form. Stir 1 tablespoon into the squash mixture; then gently fold in the remaining egg whites. Transfer the mixture to a 2-quart soufflé dish sprayed with vegetable cooking spray.

Combine the cheddar cheese, bread crumbs, and the remaining 1 tablespoon margarine. Sprinkle over top. Bake the soufflé in a 325 degree oven for 45 to 50 minutes or until the soufflé is golden brown.

Serves 8

Per serving: 195 calories, 15 grams protein, 12 grams carbohydrate, 10 grams fat (45%), 120 milligrams cholesterol, 333 milligrams sodium.

*Summer squash varieties include pattypan or scallop squash—pale green, disk-shaped; yellow or crookneck squash—yellow, cylindrical, or shaped with a bent neck; zucchini squash—dark green or striped green, long and cylindrical. Buy only firm, small summer squash. Refrigerate, unwashed, in plastic bags and use within 4 to 5 days.

GREEN BEANS WITH BLUE CHEESE & ALMONDS

This classic dish adds style to any meal. Prepare this one just before serving. Green beans are a good source of vitamins A and C and fiber. Like most vegetables, they are high in complex carbohydrates. Make sure you select crisp, not limp, beans.

- 5 cups (about 1 pound) fresh green beans, cut in 1-inch pieces
- 2 cups (about ½ pound) mushrooms, sliced
- ¼ cup green onions (white and green parts), sliced
- 2 tablespoons almonds, sliced
- 1 tablespoon dried tarragon leaves
- 2 ounces blue cheese, crumbled

In a large skillet sprayed with vegetable cooking spray, combine green beans, mushrooms, green onions, almonds, and tarragon. Sauté until green beans are tender, but firm (about 3 to 4 minutes). Add blue cheese and stir just until cheese begins to melt. Serve immediately.

Serves 6

Per serving: 81 calories, 5 grams protein, 9 grams carbohydrate, 4 grams fat (38%), 8 milligrams cholesterol, 112 milligrams sodium.

WHOLE-WHEAT POTATO BREAD

Serve this great prepare-ahead yeast bread warm with orange marmalade or your favorite topping.

3 ½ cups all-purpose flour
1 ½ cups mashed potato flakes
2 ½ teaspoons salt
  2 packages dry yeast
1 ½ cups water
1 ¼ cups low-fat milk
  ¼ cup margarine
  ¼ cup honey
  2 eggs
2 ½-3 ½ cups whole-wheat flour

In a large bowl, combine 1 ½ cups of the all-purpose flour, the potato flakes, salt, and yeast. Blend well.

In a medium saucepan, heat water, milk, margarine, and honey until very warm (120 to 130 degrees). Add warm liquid and eggs to flour mixture. At low speed of an electric mixer, blend until moistened.

At medium speed, beat an additional 4 minutes. By hand, stir in the remaining all-purpose flour and 1 ½ to 2 cups of the whole-wheat flour until dough pulls away from sides of bowl.

On a floured surface, knead in remaining whole-wheat flour until dough feels smooth and elastic (about 10 minutes). Place dough in a bowl sprayed with vegetable cooking spray. Cover it loosely with plastic wrap and cloth towel. Set in a warm place (80 to 85 degrees) to rise until double in size (about 1 hour).

Punch dough down. Divide into 2 parts and shape each into a ball. Let dough set on counter, covered with inverted bowl, for 15 minutes. Shape dough into 2 loaves and place in 2 (5-by-9-inch) loaf pans. Cover and set in a warm place to rise until double in size (30 to 45 minutes).

Bake at 375 degrees for 35 to 40 minutes until golden brown. Remove from pans.

Makes 2 loaves (15 slices per loaf)
Per slice: 157 calories, 4 grams protein, 31 grams carbohydrate, 2 grams fat (12%), less than 1 milligram cholesterol, 216 milligrams sodium.

GOOD EARTH SALAD

I first tasted this version of tabbouleh—a Middle Eastern dish—at a Registered Dietitian's conference last year. The mint adds a cool touch to the hearty grains and legumes. Any way you spell tabbouleh (there are about 10 ways), this tastes great!

1 cup dried bulgur wheat
1 cup dried lentils, rinsed and drained
¼ teaspoon salt
3 tablespoons lemon juice
¼ cup olive oil
½ teaspoon dried mint leaves
1 teaspoon dried oregano leaves
3-4 green onions (white and green parts), sliced
2 medium cucumbers, peeled, seeded, and chopped
½ each red and yellow bell pepper, minced
2 fresh tomatoes, diced
1 cup fresh or frozen green peas
1 cup fresh parsley, chopped

In a medium bowl, combine bulgur with 2 cups boiling water. Cover and let stand for 30 minutes.

In a medium saucepan, add lentils to at least 3 cups boiling water. Simmer without stirring until lentils are tender (about 20 to 30 minutes). Check frequently and add more water, if necessary. When lentils are tender, drain and then rinse them in cold water.

Combine salt, lemon juice, oil, mint, and oregano. Add pepper, if desired, to taste. Toss with bulgur and lentils. Chill until ready to serve.

Just before serving, toss bulgur mixture with green onions, cucumbers, bell peppers, tomatoes, green peas, and parsley. Adjust seasonings.

Serves 10
Per serving: 194 calories, 8 grams protein, 29 grams carbohydrate, 6 grams fat (27%), 0 milligrams cholesterol, 61 milligrams sodium.

Do you think that the things people make fools of themselves about are any less real and true than the things they behave sensibly about?
—GEORGE BERNARD SHAW

BLUEBERRY CHEESECAKE

In keeping with the rest of the menu, this finale is light and colorful. When I serve it to friends, they can't believe that it is so low in fat.

- ¾ cup graham cracker crumbs (about 18 squares)
- 3 tablespoons reduced-calorie margarine
- 2 envelopes unflavored gelatin
- 1 cup low-fat milk
- 4 eggs
- 1 ½ cups sugar, divided
- 3 cups low-fat cottage cheese
- 8 ounces reduced-calorie cream cheese
- 2 teaspoons vanilla extract
- 2 tablespoons cornstarch
- 2 tablespoons lemon juice
- 1 cup water
- 3 cups fresh blueberries
- *garnish:* lemon rind strips

Combine graham cracker crumbs and margarine; stir well. Firmly press crumb mixture into bottom of a 9-inch springform pan sprayed with vegetable cooking spray. Bake at 375 degrees for 5 minutes. Let cool slightly; then chill.

In a medium microwave-safe bowl, sprinkle gelatin over milk. Let stand for a minute until gelatin softens. Beat in eggs and 1 cup of the sugar. Microwave on HIGH for 3 minutes, stirring every minute, until creamy. Then beat until smooth.

In a food processor or electric blender, combine cottage cheese and cream cheese. Process until smooth (about 5 minutes). Add the custard mixture and blend well. Add the vanilla and blend well.

Pour into prepared graham cracker crust. Refrigerate until set (about 2 hours).

In a small saucepan, combine cornstarch and lemon juice. Stir until cornstarch is dissolved. Add the remaining ½ cup sugar and water. Bring to a boil. Then reduce heat and simmer, stirring constantly, until sauce thickens. Add blueberries and stir gently. Remove from heat and let cool.

When ready to serve, remove cake from springform pan. Top with blueberry sauce and garnish with lemon rind.

Serves 16

Per serving: 223 calories, 10 grams protein, 30 grams carbohydrate, 7 grams fat (28%), 73 milligrams cholesterol, 225 milligrams sodium.

UNDER THE STARS

Last year, it seemed as if we were eating the same things every time we left the city and headed for the hills. So, I created these prepare-ahead recipes and, fortunately for me, my family enjoys them. Be sure to bring along Dutch ovens and pans for heating, big spoons and ladles, and hearty appetites. Add some novelty by including these recipes in your next camping trip, even if that is in your own backyard!

ᔥ

M·E·N·U

Minestrone Soup
•
Greek Salad–Filled French Bread Round
•
Rice & Red Beans
•
Granola
•
Apricot Cider

MINESTRONE SOUP

This full-bodied soup will warm your insides on those cold nights in the tent. Prepare this one before you go so that the flavors will blend.

- 6 cups water
- 2 tablespoons olive oil
- 1 medium onion, chopped
- 2 cloves garlic, minced
- 2 large leeks (white and 1 inch of green parts), sliced
- 1 ½ cups (2 large) carrots, chopped
- 2 ½ cups (½ pound) green beans, cut into 1-inch pieces
- 1 large potato, unpeeled and diced
- 1 (15-ounce) can tomato sauce
- 1 (14 ½-ounce) can Italian-style stewed tomatoes, undrained
- 2 cups (½ pound) zucchini, thinly sliced
- ½ cup cabbage, chopped
- 1 (15-ounce) can kidney beans, rinsed and drained
- 4 ounces small shell pasta
- 2 tablespoons dried parsley
- 1 teaspoon dried basil leaves
- *garnish:* Parmesan cheese

In a large pot, bring the water to a boil.

Meanwhile, in a Dutch oven, heat the oil. Add the onion, garlic, leeks, carrots, and green beans. Sauté the vegetables for about 5 minutes. Then add the potato, boiling water, tomato sauce, and stewed tomatoes. Bring to a boil; reduce the heat. Simmer the soup, uncovered, for about 30 minutes.

Add the zucchini, cabbage, beans, and pasta. Bring the soup back to a boil, reduce the heat, and simmer until the pasta is cooked.

Add the parsley and basil. Adjust seasonings with salt and pepper, if desired, to taste. Garnish with grated Parmesan cheese.

Serves 12
Per serving: 131 calories, 5 grams protein, 23 grams carbohydrate, 3 grams fat (18%), 0 milligrams cholesterol, 279 milligrams sodium.

GREEK SALAD–FILLED FRENCH BREAD ROUND

This recipe is a hit with my family. The sandwich packs well, but must be kept cold. If you do not have time to bake the French bread, bakeries or supermarkets supply good-tasting French bread rounds. Why are appetites especially big when people are out of doors?

  1 small head romaine lettuce, torn into bite-size pieces
  1 cup cooked garbanzo beans
  ½ each red, yellow, and green bell pepper, sliced julienne
  ⅓ cup red onion, sliced
  6 cherry tomatoes, halved
 10 black olives
French Bread Round (see following recipe)

Feta Dressing:
  1 ounce feta cheese
  2 tablespoons fresh lemon juice
  1 tablespoon olive oil
  1 clove garlic, minced
  1 teaspoon dried oregano leaves
  ¼ teaspoon sugar
  ⅛ teaspoon ground pepper (optional)

In a large bowl, combine lettuce, garbanzo beans, pepper strips, red onion, tomatoes, and olives.

For the Feta Dressing: Process all ingredients in food processor or electric blender until smooth.

Cut French Bread Round in half horizontally. Hollow out the soft bread from both halves, leaving a shell about ½- to ¾-inch thick. Spray cut edges of bread with olive oil–flavored vegetable cooking spray.

Spoon salad into the shell; drizzle dressing over salad. Cover with top half of bread, pressing firmly. Seal the sandwich tightly in plastic wrap first and then foil. Chill.

When ready to serve, press firmly on the wrapped sandwich to flatten it. Unwrap and cut into wedges.

Serves 6
Per serving: 110 calories, 4 grams protein, 12 grams carbohydrate, 6 grams fat (44%), 4 milligrams cholesterol, 119 milligrams sodium.

FRENCH BREAD ROUND

Feel like an accomplished baker as you make this simple yeast bread. On another occasion, roll the dough out into a rectangle; beginning with a long side, roll jelly-roll style; allow to rise; make slash marks on the diagonal; bake.

  1 package dry yeast
  1 cup warm water (105 to 115 degrees)
  2 cups all-purpose flour
1 ½ teaspoons salt, divided
  ½ cup cake flour*
      cornmeal
  1 egg

Dissolve yeast in warm water and let stand until foamy (about 10 minutes).

Put all-purpose flour and 1 teaspoon salt in a food processor fitted with a steel knife. With the machine running, add yeast mixture in a thin stream through the feed tube. Mix about 40 to 50 seconds or until dough is elastic and smooth.

Place in a mixing bowl sprayed with vegetable cooking spray. Turn dough in bowl to coat entire surface. Cover with a damp towel and let rise in a warm place until double (about 1 hour). Punch down.

Turn dough out onto a heavily floured board; work in cake flour to make dough easy to handle and not sticky. Roll dough into a ball. Place on pie plate sprayed with vegetable cooking spray and sprinkled with cornmeal. Cover again with a damp towel and let rise until double (about 45 minutes).

Beat egg lightly with remaining salt. Brush over top of loaf. Bake at 425 degrees for 30 to 35 minutes until golden brown.

Makes 1 loaf
Per ⅙ round (not hollowed): 279 calories, 10 grams protein, 50 grams carbohydrate, 4 grams fat (12%), 137 milligrams cholesterol, 570 milligrams sodium.

*½ cup sifted all-purpose flour minus 1 tablespoon flour plus 1 tablespoon cornstarch makes ½ cup sifted cake flour.

Poems are made by fools like me, But only God can make a tree.
—(ALFRED) JOYCE KILMER

Rice & Red Beans

Combining rice with red beans is a classic recipe in the South. Here is my version with a few more vegetables added for color. There's nothing nicer than a bowl of warm beans and rice while singing songs by the campfire.

1 tablespoon vegetable oil
1 medium onion, chopped
2 cloves garlic, finely minced
2 medium tomatoes, finely diced
1 cup (about 1 medium) green pepper, chopped
1 cup (about 3 stalks) celery, sliced
½ teaspoon dried oregano leaves
1 (15-ounce) can red beans, rinsed and drained
4 cups cooked brown rice

Heat the oil in a large skillet; add the onion and garlic. Sauté until soft.

Add the tomatoes, green pepper, celery, and oregano. Cover the skillet; simmer the mixture for about 5 minutes or until the vegetables are crisp-tender.

Add the beans and simmer, stirring occasionally, until heated through. Add salt and pepper, if desired, to taste.

When ready to serve, spoon the vegetable-bean mixture over the rice.

Serves 8

Per serving: 220 calories, 8 grams protein, 42 grams carbohydrate, 3 grams fat (11%), 0 milligrams cholesterol, 20 milligrams sodium.

Apricot Cider

It's cold in them thar hills! Take something to warm your tummy and your toes. Heat the cider over the campfire for a late nightcap.

1 quart apricot nectar
2 cups unsweetened apple juice
2 cups unsweetened pineapple juice
1 orange, sliced
1 lemon, sliced
4 large cinnamon sticks
6 whole cloves

Granola

Isn't it true that camping and granola go together like hand and glove? Most granolas are too high in fat (especially tropical fats, such as coconut and palm oils) and usually are too sweet. My daughter, Meredith, can't get enough of this crunchy concoction.

3 tablespoons reduced-calorie margarine, melted
¼ cup brown sugar, packed
1 ½ cups rolled oats
½ cup wheat bran
½ cup whole-wheat flour
½ cup sesame seeds
¼ cup sunflower seeds, untoasted
¼ cup almonds or walnuts, chopped
1 teaspoon ground cinnamon
1 cup raisins
½ cup dried apricots, chopped

In a 9-by-13-inch baking pan, combine the margarine and the brown sugar.

Add remaining ingredients, except the raisins and apricots. Bake the mixture in a preheated 350 degree oven for about 25 to 30 minutes or until the mixture is lightly browned, stirring it several times.

Remove from oven and stir in the raisins and apricots. Cool completely before transferring to a large storage container.

Makes about 3 cups

Per 2-ounce serving: 226 calories, 7 grams protein, 33 grams carbohydrate, 10 grams fat (38%), 0 milligrams cholesterol, 28 milligrams sodium.

¼ teaspoon ground nutmeg
¼ teaspoon ground ginger

In a large saucepan, combine all the ingredients; bring mixture to a boil. Reduce heat to low and simmer the cider for 30 to 40 minutes. Strain and serve hot.

Makes about 8 cups

Per cup: 133 calories, less than 1 gram protein, 34 grams carbohydrate, less than 1 gram fat (1%), 0 milligrams cholesterol, 9 milligrams sodium.

GLORIOUS GARDENS

I am not a great gardener, but my attempts to grow vegetables have been fun for the family—mostly for my children. They always ask, "How can this little seed make such a big plant?" That leap of faith is pretty exciting when you're a kid.

∾

CHILLED GREEN BEAN BISQUE

Refreshing and colorful are words to describe this beautiful green soup. Try to use the freshest green beans for the best flavor.

2   tablespoons reduced-calorie margarine
1   clove garlic, minced
1   medium onion, chopped
4   cups (1 pound) fresh green beans, cut into 1-inch pieces
3   cups Vegetable Broth (see p. 91)
1   cup low-fat milk
¼   teaspoon dried savory leaves
½   teaspoon dried dill weed
✄   *garnish:* plain low-fat yogurt and sliced almonds

In a Dutch oven, melt margarine over medium heat. Add garlic and onion; sauté until translucent. Stir in beans and broth. Cover and simmer until beans are crisp-tender (about 10 minutes).

Pour mixture into a food processor or electric blender. Process until smooth. Return to saucepan. Add milk and stir well.

Season with savory and dill weed. Add ¼ teaspoon salt and pepper, if desired, or to taste. Cover and chill well.

To serve, pour into chilled mugs or bowls. Top each with a dollop of yogurt and a sprinkle of sliced almonds.

Makes about 6 cups

Per 1 cup serving: 99 calories, 6 grams protein, 11 grams carbohydrate, 4 grams fat (33%), 3 milligrams cholesterol, 452 milligrams sodium.

M·E·N·U

Chilled Green Bean Bisque

•

Garden-Topped Potatoes

•

Tofu–Snap Pea Salad & Creamy Herb Dressing

•

Sun Country Tomato Salad

•

Spiced Couscous in Cantaloupe

•

Fresh Raspberry Yogurt in Cookie Baskets

✂ GARDEN-TOPPED POTATOES

This recipe is similar to a dish I had at Cafe Pierpont, a fabulous restaurant in Salt Lake City, Utah. The vegetable combinations impressed me. And this dish is very simple to prepare.

2 cups cooked pinto beans or 1 (15-ounce) can pinto beans
1 (1.5-ounce) package taco seasoning mix
1 (8-ounce) can tomato sauce
1 cup broccoli florets
1 medium carrot, sliced julienne
1 cup fresh or frozen corn kernels
8 medium russet potatoes, baked
1 medium cucumber, peeled, seeded, and sliced julienne
5-6 green onions (white and green parts), sliced
1 cup low-fat cottage cheese
1 cup part-skim mozzarella cheese, grated
1 cup purchased salsa or Gazpacho Dip (see p. 76)

In a large saucepan, combine pinto beans, taco seasoning mix, and tomato sauce. Heat until boiling; then simmer for 15 minutes.

Combine broccoli, carrot, and corn; place in a microwave-safe bowl. Microwave on HIGH for 4 minutes or until vegetables are crisp-tender. Keep warm.

When ready to serve, top baked potatoes with bean mixture, vegetable mixture, cucumber, green onions, cottage cheese, mozzarella cheese, and salsa or Gazpacho Dip (see p. 76).

Serves 8
Per serving: 357 calories, 20 grams protein, 56 grams carbohydrate, 6 grams fat (16%), 17 milligrams cholesterol, 429 milligrams sodium.

♣ TOFU–SNAP PEA SALAD & CREAMY HERB DRESSING

Rebecca Robison, our talented food stylist, introduced this refreshing recipe to me. I altered the dressing recipe to reduce the fat content without diminishing the great taste.

8 ounces tofu, cubed
1 Red Delicious apple, unpeeled and cubed
1 medium cucumber, unpeeled and diced
1 medium zucchini, sliced julienne
2 cups mung bean sprouts
2 ½ cups (½ pound) fresh snap peas, cut into 1-inch pieces
2-3 green onions (white and green parts), sliced
½ cup celery, sliced
3 tablespoons Herb Dressing Mix (see recipe below)
¼ cup reduced-calorie mayonnaise
¼ cup plain low-fat yogurt
½ cup buttermilk

Herb Dressing Mix:
¼ cup dried parsley
3 tablespoons dried minced onion
1 tablespoon dried chives
1 teaspoon salt
½ teaspoon garlic powder
½ teaspoon ground celery seed
¼ teaspoon black pepper (optional)

In a large bowl, combine tofu, apple, and vegetables.

For the dressing: Combine the dressing mix ingredients in a small jar and mix well. Store in a dry place.

Combine 3 tablespoons Herb Dressing Mix with mayonnaise and yogurt; mix thoroughly with a wire whisk. Add the buttermilk gradually, stirring constantly, until well mixed. Chill.

When ready to serve, combine salad with dressing; toss gently.

Serves 8
Per serving: 106 calories, 5 grams protein, 13 grams carbohydrate, 4 grams fat (35%), 3 milligrams cholesterol, 112 milligrams sodium.

Sun Country Tomato Salad

Probably nothing is tastier than fresh tomatoes from the garden. The colors in this recipe will impress your guests. The flavor will keep them coming back for more. If you use the jalapeño pepper, wear gloves or wash hands thoroughly because of its volatile oils. Do not touch your face or eyes while preparing it.

5-6 cups (1 ½ pounds) ripe cherry tomatoes*
   5 medium-size (about 1-inch diameter) tomatilloes
   1 fresh jalapeño pepper, seeded and minced (optional)
   ¼ cup fresh cilantro leaves, lightly packed
   ¼ cup lime juice
   garnish: lime wedges

Stem cherry tomatoes; rinse and drain. Halve tomatoes larger than ¾-inch diameter.

Remove tomatillo husks; rinse well, core, and thinly slice.

Gently mix tomatoes with tomatilloes, jalapeño pepper, cilantro, and lime juice. Add salt and pepper, if desired, to taste. Garnish with lime wedges.

Serves 8

Per serving: 23 calories, 1 gram protein, 5 grams carbohydrate, less than 1 gram fat (8%), 0 milligrams cholesterol, 9 milligrams sodium.

*For cherry tomatoes, use red, yellow-green, and/or orange; include some ½-inch or less in diameter.

Spiced Couscous in Cantaloupe

Enjoy a delicious fiber boost with this side dish. Did you know that cantaloupe is one of the most healthful fruits around? It is loaded with vitamins A and C, especially important for your skin during these sunny summer months.

1 ⅓ cups water
   ½ teaspoon ground cinnamon
   ½ cup couscous
   1 large cantaloupe
   1 cup fruit-flavored low-fat yogurt
   ⅓ cup dry-roasted peanuts, chopped
   ¼ cup golden raisins
   2 tablespoons fresh mint, minced
   garnish: fresh mint sprigs

In a 1 ½- to 2-quart saucepan, bring water and cinnamon to a boil over high heat. Add couscous and stir well. Cover and remove pan from heat. Let stand until water is completely absorbed (about 5 minutes). Remove lid to allow couscous to cool.

While couscous cools, cut cantaloupe lengthwise into 6 wedges; scoop out and discard seeds.

Mix cooled couscous with yogurt, peanuts, raisins, and minced mint. Spoon couscous mixture into cavity of each cantaloupe wedge. Garnish with mint sprigs.

Makes 6 servings

Per serving: 174 calories, 6 grams protein, 29 grams carbohydrate, 4 grams fat (22%), 2 milligrams cholesterol, 62 milligrams sodium.

A Garden is a lovesome thing, God wot!
—T. E. BROWN

❧ FRESH RASPBERRY YOGURT IN COOKIE BASKETS

My children and I always look forward to fresh raspberries when we visit Grandma. The berries, however, never make it back to the house because we eat them as soon as we pick them!

1 envelope unflavored gelatin
3 tablespoons water
2 cups fresh raspberries, divided
1 cup evaporated low-fat milk
1 (8-ounce) carton plain low-fat yogurt
¼ cup sugar
❧ *garnish:* fresh mint sprigs

In a medium saucepan, sprinkle gelatin over water; let stand 1 minute until gelatin is softened. Cook over medium heat, stirring until gelatin dissolves. Remove from heat.

Combine 1 cup raspberries, milk, yogurt, and sugar. Stir into gelatin mixture. Spoon into an 8-inch square pan; freeze until firm.

Remove from freezer and break into pieces. Spoon mixture into a medium bowl; beat at medium speed of an electric mixer until smooth. Return mixture to pan; freeze until firm.

When ready to serve, let the yogurt stand at room temperature to soften (about 10 minutes). Spoon into cookie baskets and top with remaining 1 cup raspberries. Garnish with mint sprigs.

Serves 6
Per serving: 120 calories, 6 grams protein, 24 grams carbohydrate, 1 gram fat (8%), 3 milligrams cholesterol, 67 milligrams sodium.

COOKIE BASKETS

These little baskets will delight your guests. They can be made ahead of time for a quick summer dessert. For a variation, roll warm cookies into tight scrolls. Because this recipe is very high in fat, serve it with the very low fat yogurt for an overall healthful dessert.

¼ cup blanched almonds
⅓ cup cake flour*
¼ cup margarine
½ cup sugar
2 egg whites
¼ teaspoon almond extract

In a food processor or electric blender, process almonds until they resemble coarse flour.

In a small bowl, combine almond powder and flour. Set aside.

In a medium bowl, cream margarine and sugar until fluffy. Add egg whites and blend well. Stir in extract. Gradually add flour mixture; beat until smooth.

Prepare two baskets at a time. Drop batter by the level tablespoon onto baking sheets sprayed with vegetable cooking spray. Space about 3 inches apart. With a spatula, flatten dough to a 4-inch diameter. Bake in a preheated 400 degree oven for 4 to 6 minutes or until edges begin to turn brown.

Working quickly, cool cookie only until it is firm enough to handle (about 30 seconds to 1 minute). Remove with a spatula and drape over a 3-inch-diameter drinking glass; press outside of cookie into glass to form basket. If cookie becomes too hard to mold, return to oven for about 1 minute to soften. When set, transfer baskets to wire rack. Repeat with remaining dough.

Makes 6 baskets
Per basket: 192 calories, 3 grams protein, 23 grams carbohydrate, 11 grams fat (50%), 0 milligrams cholesterol, 117 milligrams sodium.

*⅓ cup sifted all-purpose flour minus 2 teaspoons flour plus 2 teaspoons cornstarch makes ⅓ cup sifted cake flour.

FREEDOM

Summer is picnic time with tables set up under big shade trees and ice cream freezers churning. Children display newly learned gymnastic tricks for proud grandparents. This picnic menu offers unique versions of traditional favorites, along with new ideas for preparing vegetables.

℮ BLACK & WHITE BEAN SALAD WITH FETA CHEESE

Plan ahead. The black beans must be soaked, cooked, and marinated. But from there, this salad is a snap to make.

2	cups dried black beans
1	cup cooked garbanzo beans
4	ounces feta cheese, crumbled
¼	cup red onion, minced
¼	cup green onions (white and green parts), sliced
⅓	cup fresh mint leaves, tightly packed and finely chopped
¼	cup olive oil
3	tablespoons fresh lemon juice
2	tablespoons sugar
1	teaspoon garlic powder
1	teaspoon celery seed

In a large pot, cover washed black beans with water and soak overnight or at least 8 hours. Drain the beans. Cover soaked beans with water. Bring to a boil; reduce heat and simmer for 2 to 3 hours or until the beans are thoroughly cooked.

Place the cooked beans in a large mixing bowl. Add the garbanzo beans, feta cheese, red and green onions, and mint; toss lightly.

Combine the oil, lemon juice, sugar, garlic powder, and celery seed. Add ⅛ teaspoon salt and pepper, if desired, or to taste. Pour over mixture. Let the salad marinate in the refrigerator for ½ to 1 hour. Adjust the seasonings before serving.

Serves 8

Per serving: 173 calories, 8 grams protein, 21 grams carbohydrate, 7 grams fat (36%), 8 milligrams cholesterol, 107 milligrams sodium.

M·E·N·U

Black & White Bean Salad With Feta Cheese

•

Garden Pasta Salad & Creamy Dill Dressing

•

Sweet Onion–Potato Salad

•

Grilled Summer Vegetables

•

Watermelon Sorbet

•

Banana-Carrot Bread

Garden Pasta Salad & Creamy Dill Dressing

Pastas have become so popular that we can't keep up with the new varieties and shapes. The kids will go crazy over this bow tie–shaped pasta combined with their favorite vegetables. The abundance of complex carbohydrates provides plenty of energy for the day's activities.

3 cups bow tie pasta, cooked and drained
1 cup (2 medium) carrots, grated
1 cup (1 stalk) broccoli florets
½ cup celery, thinly sliced
½ cup red bell pepper, seeded and diced
½ cup green bell pepper, seeded and diced
½ cup cucumber, peeled, seeded, and diced
¼ cup fresh parsley, chopped
2-3 green onions (white and green parts), sliced

Creamy Dill Dressing:
⅔ cup plain low-fat yogurt
¼ cup reduced-calorie mayonnaise
2 tablespoons fresh lemon juice or red wine vinegar
2 teaspoons dried dill weed
¼ teaspoon garlic powder

In a medium bowl, combine all salad ingredients; stir well.

For the dressing: In a small bowl, blend all dressing ingredients with wire whisk. Add ¼ teaspoon salt and pepper, if desired, or to taste. Chill.

When ready to serve, combine salad mixture with dressing. Toss lightly.

Serves 10
Per serving: 101 calories, 3 grams protein, 16 grams carbohydrate, 3 grams fat (24%), 3 milligrams cholesterol, 40 milligrams sodium.

Sweet Onion–Potato Salad

A good friend, who is well known for her healthful cooking, shared this terrific recipe at a potluck picnic. If we all could look like Diane by eating this potato salad, we would say, "More, more, more!"

3 pounds medium-size red potatoes
1 large sweet white onion, quartered and thinly sliced
¾ cup celery, thinly sliced
1 large Golden Delicious apple, cored and diced
¼ cup black olives, diced
⅓ cup sweet pickle, chopped
1 cup plain low-fat yogurt
½ cup reduced-calorie mayonnaise
2 teaspoons Dijon mustard (optional)
2 tablespoons fresh lemon juice
1 teaspoon reduced-sodium soy sauce

Boil potatoes until tender (about 30 minutes). Drain. Dice when cool.

Add onion, celery, apple, olives, and pickles.

In a small bowl, combine yogurt, mayonnaise, mustard, lemon juice, and soy sauce. Add salt and pepper, if desired, to taste. Mix gently. Fold into potato mixture. Cover and chill at least 4 hours.

Serves 10
Per serving: 210 calories, 4 grams protein, 38 grams carbohydrate, 6 grams fat (24%), 5 milligrams cholesterol, 194 milligrams sodium.

*Hold fast to dreams
For when dreams go
Life is a barren field
Frozen with snow.*
—LANGSTON HUGHES

GRILLED SUMMER VEGETABLES

Summer picnics or parties are the perfect setting for grilling outdoors. Cook vegetables over medium to medium-hot heat on a covered grill. Because vegetables dry out easily, be sure to marinate beforehand and/or baste frequently throughout cooking. The mushrooms marinate for at least 8 hours in this recipe; plan accordingly. Microwave or steam vegetables before grilling to speed up cooking time.

Mushroom Marinade:
- ¼ cup olive oil
- 2 tablespoons lemon juice
- 2 cloves garlic, minced
- ¼ teaspoon dried tarragon leaves
- ¼ teaspoon salt

Herbed Margarine:
- ½ cup reduced-calorie margarine, melted
- ¼ cup green onions (white and green parts), chopped
- 1 tablespoon dried basil leaves
- 1 tablespoon dried parsley
- 1 teaspoon lemon-pepper seasoning
- 1 teaspoon garlic powder

- 8 large fresh mushrooms
- 8 small red new potatoes, scrubbed
- 4 ears of fresh corn, broken in halves
- 4 small summer squash (choose from zucchini, pattypan, and/or yellow crookneck), cut into chunks
- 2 green peppers, seeded and quartered
- 1 small eggplant, cut into ¼-inch-thick slices
- 2 red onions, quartered
- 8 red cherry tomatoes, stemmed

For the Mushroom Marinade: In a small bowl, combine ingredients and mix well.

For the Herbed Margarine: In a medium bowl, combine ingredients and mix well.

Add mushrooms to the Mushroom Marinade. Cover and chill for at least 8 hours.

Place potatoes in a microwave-safe bowl. Microwave on HIGH for 6 to 7 minutes or until tender.

Remove husks and silks from corn just before grilling. Brush Herbed Margarine on vegetables, coating well.

Place each ear of corn on a piece of heavy-duty aluminum foil. Roll foil lengthwise around each ear; twist foil at each end. Grill corn, covered, over medium coals for 20 minutes, turning after 10 minutes.

Thread the potatoes, squash, green peppers, eggplant, onions, and tomatoes onto 16- to 18-inch skewers. Grill them over hot coals, turning and basting frequently with the Herbed Margarine until lightly browned (about 12 to 15 minutes).

Serves 8
Per serving: 193 calories, 4 grams protein, 30 grams carbohydrate, 8 grams fat (34%), 0 milligrams cholesterol, 93 milligrams sodium.

WATERMELON SORBET

Instead of watermelon wedges at this year's picnic, try this refreshing sorbet for dessert.

- 10 cups watermelon, seeded and cubed
- ⅔ cup sugar
- 1 ½ cups unsweetened apple juice
- ½ cup fresh lemon juice

Place half of watermelon in container of food processor or electric blender. Process until smooth. Pour purée into a large bowl; repeat procedure with remaining watermelon.

In a small saucepan, combine sugar, apple juice, and lemon juice; cook over medium heat, stirring until sugar dissolves. Remove from heat; let cool.

Combine puréed watermelon with apple juice mixture; mix well. Pour into a 9-by-13-inch pan; freeze until almost firm.

Transfer mixture to a large mixing bowl; beat at medium speed of an electric mixer until smooth. Return mixture to pan; freeze until firm.

Let stand at room temperature for 10 minutes before serving.

Makes 12 servings
Per 6-ounce serving: 101 calories, 1 gram protein, 25 grams carbohydrate, less than 1 gram fat (5%), 0 milligrams cholesterol, 5 milligrams sodium.

❧
BANANA-CARROT BREAD

This bread is surprisingly moist because of the amount of grated carrot. Top with reduced-calorie cream cheese for a richer taste.

  1 cup whole-wheat flour
  1 cup all-purpose flour
  1 teaspoon baking powder
  1 teaspoon baking soda
  ½ teaspoon cinnamon
  ¼ teaspoon salt
  ⅛ teaspoon ground cloves
  ¼ cup margarine
  ¾ cup brown sugar
  1 egg, lightly beaten
  2 egg whites, lightly beaten
  2 large bananas, very ripe, peeled and mashed
1 ¼ teaspoons vanilla extract
  2 large carrots, finely grated
  ½ cup walnuts, chopped

Preheat oven to 350 degrees.

In a large bowl, combine flours, baking powder, baking soda, cinnamon, salt, and cloves.

In a medium bowl, cream margarine and brown sugar. Beat in egg, egg whites, bananas, and vanilla. Add banana mixture to dry ingredients; stir in carrots and walnuts.

Pour into a 5-by-9-inch loaf pan sprayed with vegetable cooking spray. Bake for 1 hour or until knife inserted in center of loaf comes out clean.

Makes 1 loaf (15 slices)

Per slice: 166 calories, 4 grams protein, 28 grams carbohydrate, 5 grams fat (26%), 18 milligrams cholesterol, 157 milligrams sodium.

FIESTA AND SIESTA

When days are full and I have so much to do, I wish I didn't have to sleep. But most of the time, I am grateful for rest. Our bodies need to recharge. Asleep, awake, asleep, awake is perhaps the simplest cycle in life. It's almost like a fiesta and siesta.

I really like Mexican cuisine. And summer days are perfect for this zesty, moist, and colorful fare. Make the meal memorable by inviting friends to wear Mexican attire; decorate with bright paper flowers, piñatas, and lanterns.

CARIBBEAN QUENCHER

Quench your warm-weather thirst with this refreshing fruit slush. Select the ripest mango and papaya you can find in order to get the sweetest flavor and smoothest texture.

1 ½ cups (about 1 medium) mango, peeled and chopped
1 ½ cups (about 1 medium) papaya, peeled and chopped
1 ½ cups water
  2 teaspoons lime juice
  ½ teaspoon coconut flavoring (optional)
  ½ cup frozen guava-pineapple-orange juice concentrate, undiluted
  garnish: lime and lemon wedges

Combine all ingredients except garnish in container of an electric blender; process until smooth. Pour into a 9-by-13-inch pan; cover and freeze 3 hours or until slushy. Spoon into individual glasses. Garnish with lime and lemon wedges.

Makes 5 cups
Per ½ cup: 112 calories, 1 gram protein, 28 grams carbohydrate, less than 1 gram fat (2%), 0 milligrams cholesterol, 5 milligrams sodium.

RICE ACAPULCO

Rice is a staple food of Mexican cuisine. This recipe is full of flavorful vegetables and spices that add a Latin touch.

  1 onion, finely diced
  1 green pepper, finely diced
  1 clove garlic, minced
1 ½ cups long-grain white rice
  2 tablespoons olive oil
  2 cups tomatoes, peeled and diced
  3 cups Vegetable Broth (see p. 91)
  1 teaspoon ground cumin
  1 teaspoon dried oregano leaves
  1 teaspoon paprika

In a large saucepan, sauté onion, green pepper, garlic, and rice in heated oil until rice is golden.

Add remaining ingredients; stir and bring to a boil.

Simmer, covered, until rice is cooked (about 20 minutes).

Serves 8
Per serving: 148 calories, 4 grams protein, 23 grams carbohydrate, 4 grams fat (25%), less than 1 milligram cholesterol, 297 milligrams sodium.

M·E·N·U

Caribbean Quencher
•
Rice Acapulco
•
Mexican Vegetables
&
Gazpacho Dip
•
Enchiladas Monterey
•
Apricot-Cilantro Salad
•
Flan

BACK TO SCHOOL

My mother-in-law once said, "We raise our children to leave us." Our schools play a big part in this preparation process. A good education leaves us socially, emotionally, intellectually, and physically prepared to make it on our own. And now, when I hear the school bell ring, I am reminded of those pleasant and painful years of learning and growing. I am glad they are behind me.

♣

CORN CHOWDER

Children love sweet corn, especially in a soup that warms during chilly fall weather. Most corn chowders are high in cholesterol-rich fat. Just as flavorful, this recipe is considerably lower in fat.

2 tablespoons reduced-calorie margarine
1 clove garlic, minced
1 medium onion, chopped
2 medium potatoes, scrubbed and diced
2 cups celery, sliced
4 cups (about 8 ears) fresh corn kernels or 2 (10-ounce) packages frozen whole-kernel corn
4 cups Vegetable Broth (see p. 91)
2 tablespoons fresh thyme, coarsely chopped, or 1 teaspoon dried thyme leaves
12 ounces evaporated low-fat milk
❧ *garnish:* tomato, peeled, seeded, and chopped

In a heavy saucepan, melt margarine; add garlic and onion; sauté until onion is translucent.

Add potatoes, celery, corn, and vegetable broth; bring mixture to a boil. Cover, reduce heat; simmer 20 minutes or until vegetables are tender; remove from heat.

If a smooth texture is desired, place soup in a food processor or electric blender. Process mixture until smooth. Return to soup pot.

Add ¼ teaspoon salt and pepper, if desired, or to taste. Add thyme. Stir in milk; adjust seasonings. When ready to serve, top with chopped tomato.

Serves 8

Per 1 ½ cup serving: 184 calories, 9 grams protein, 33 grams carbohydrate, 3 grams fat (12%), 2 milligrams cholesterol, 492 milligrams sodium.

M·E·N·U

Corn Chowder
•
Cabbage-Apple Salad
&
Sweet Savory Dressing
•
Pita Pizzas
•
Chunky
Apple & Peanut Butter
Cookies
•
50-50 Shake

CABBAGE-APPLE SALAD & SWEET SAVORY DRESSING

This is a colorful, pleasing salad. The children will enjoy the toasted nuts and the sweetness of the dressing. You will appreciate the vitamin C in the cabbage. Each serving just about meets a child's entire Recommended Daily Allowance of vitamin C.

- 3 cups red cabbage, shredded
- 3 cups green cabbage, shredded
- 4 green onions (white and green parts), sliced
- 1 medium carrot, peeled and grated
- 2 medium apples, cored and diced
- ½ cup raisins
- ¼ cup sunflower seeds, toasted
- ¼ cup slivered almonds, toasted

Dressing:
- 3 tablespoons lemon juice
- 1 tablespoon sugar
- 1 teaspoon garlic salt
- 1 tablespoon poppy seeds

In a large bowl, combine red cabbage and green cabbage, green onions, carrot, apples, and raisins. Cover and chill.

Mix all dressing ingredients until well blended. Cover and chill.

When ready to serve, combine cabbage mixture with dressing. Top with sunflower seeds and almonds.

Serves 6
Per serving: 127 calories, 3 grams protein, 21 grams carbohydrate, 5 grams fat (30%), 0 milligrams cholesterol, 281 milligrams sodium.

PITA PIZZAS

I love getting back into a schedule with the start of school, but that means I need to organize meals more efficiently. This quick pizza variation is a big hit with the children. Experiment with whatever toppings you have on hand.

- 8 pitas (7 to 8 inches in diameter), uncut
- 1 cup of your favorite pizza sauce
- 1 cup tomatoes, seeded and chopped
- 1 cup fresh mushrooms, chopped
- 1 teaspoon dried Italian herb blend
- 1 cup part-skim mozzarella cheese, shredded
- ½ cup Parmesan cheese, grated

Preheat oven to just below broil (450 to 550 degrees). Arrange pitas on a baking sheet. Top with pizza sauce, tomatoes, mushrooms, herbs, and cheeses. Bake for about 8 minutes or until crust is crisp.

Serves 8
Per serving: 293 calories, 17 grams protein, 38 grams carbohydrate, 8 grams fat (25%), 25 milligrams cholesterol, 611 milligrams sodium.

CHUNKY APPLE & PEANUT BUTTER COOKIES

Some of my best childhood memories include the tastes and smells of freshly baked peanut butter cookies. Here is a modified version with added apple chunks, a protein punch, and a lot less fat.

- ¾ cup peanut butter
- 3 tablespoons reduced-calorie margarine
- 1 cup brown sugar, firmly packed
- 1 cup whole-wheat flour, divided
- 2 egg whites
- 2 tablespoons low-fat milk
- ½ teaspoon vanilla extract
- ½ teaspoon baking soda
- 1 cup quick-cooking rolled oats
- 2 medium apples, peeled, cored, and chopped

In a small mixer bowl, beat the peanut butter and margarine until softened. Add brown sugar, ½ cup of the flour, egg whites, milk, vanilla, and baking soda. Mix well. Stir in the remaining ½ cup flour, rolled oats, and apple.

Drop rounded tablespoonfuls of dough onto an ungreased cookie sheet. Press lightly to flatten.

Bake in a 350 degree oven for 10 to 12 minutes. Remove from the cookie sheet and cool. Store in a moisture-proof container. Cookies may be frozen for up to 6 months.

Makes 2 dozen
Per cookie: 122 calories, 4 grams protein, 16 grams carbohydrate, 5 grams fat (38%), less than 1 milligram cholesterol, 42 milligrams sodium.

♣

50-50 Shake

How about a "blast from the past"? Remember 50-50 bars—the ice cream–filled popsicles that delighted us all? This recipe captures that taste sensation in a creamy shake your kids will love today.

2 cups unsweetened cranberry cocktail
½ cup orange juice
2 cups vanilla ice milk
❧ *garnish:* orange slices

Place all ingredients in an electric blender. Process until smooth. Garnish with orange slices.

Serves 4

Per 1 cup serving: 178 calories, 3 grams protein, 36 grams carbohydrate, 3 grams fat (14%), 9 milligrams cholesterol, 55 milligrams sodium.

FOOTBALL WEATHER

We breathe a little deeper and walk a little more briskly in the crisp autumn air. The change of the weather signals much more than the onset of autumn; it also brings our grand pastime—football. Whether you're a spectator or player, you'll need plenty of easy "pack and carry" foods. Make them high-energy foods for a full afternoon at the stadium. You also will enjoy these while watching the game on television in your family room armchair.

BROCCOLI CALZONE & MARINARA SAUCE

This folded-over pizza, called calzone, can be made small and tidy for appetizers or large enough to feed the family. Fill with your favorite pizza toppings, as long as they are not too wet.

Crust:
- 1 cup whole-wheat flour
- 1 cup all-purpose flour
- ½ teaspoon salt
- ⅓ cup reduced-calorie margarine
- ½ cup cold water
  olive oil, for glaze

Filling:
- 2 teaspoons olive oil
- 1 cup broccoli florets
- 1 cup onion, chopped
- 1 tablespoon fresh rosemary, chopped, or 1 teaspoon dried rosemary leaves
- ½ cup part-skim ricotta cheese
- ¼ cup part-skim mozzarella cheese, grated
- ¼ cup cooked garbanzo beans
- 1 egg white, beaten
- 2 tablespoons Parmesan cheese, grated

Marinara Sauce:
- 2 teaspoons olive oil or salad oil
- 1 clove garlic, pressed or minced
- 1 medium onion, chopped
- 1 (1-pound) can stewed tomatoes
- ¼ cup fresh basil or 1 tablespoon dried basil leaves
- 1 teaspoon dried oregano leaves
- ¼ teaspoon salt

For the dough: Combine flours and salt in medium bowl. With pastry blender, cut in margarine until dough resembles size of peas. Gradually add cold water, mixing with fork until dough clings together. Pat dough into ball, cover, and chill for 20 minutes.

For the filling: Heat the oil in a 10-inch skillet over medium-high heat. Add the broccoli, onion, and rosemary; cook 6 minutes, stirring occasionally, until vegetables are tender. Add the ricotta and cook 3 minutes longer. Transfer vegetable mixture to a bowl and let stand until cool to the touch. Stir in the mozzarella, garbanzo beans, egg white, and Parmesan cheese until combined.

For the sauce: Heat the oil in the same skillet over medium-high heat. Sauté the garlic and onion, stirring occasionally, until onions are translucent. Add tomatoes, basil, oregano, and salt. Bring to a boil; lower heat and simmer uncovered, stirring occasionally, until sauce is very thick (about 30 minutes).

On lightly floured board, roll chilled pastry dough into 8 individual pie rounds, 6 inches wide. Reserve at least ½ cup sauce for garnish. Spoon remaining sauce and filling onto pastry rounds. Moisten pastry rims with water; then fold dough in half to cover. Crimp pastry edges with fork or fingers to seal. Brush with olive oil for shiny glaze. Cut slits in top for steam to escape.

Bake at 350 degrees until crust is a rich, golden brown (about 20 minutes). Serve with remaining Marinara Sauce.

Serves 8
Per serving: 242 calories, 9 grams protein, 32 grams carbohydrate, 9 grams fat (34%), 5 milligrams cholesterol, 288 milligrams sodium.

MENU

Broccoli Calzone
&
Marinara Sauce
•
Apple-Nut Salad
&
Tofu-Honey Dressing
•
Three-Bean Salad
With
Artichoke Hearts
•
Grape Cider
•
Apricot-Raisin Bars

APPLE-NUT SALAD &
TOFU-HONEY DRESSING

*The voice of the last
cricket
across the first frost
is one kind of goodbye.*
—CARL SANDBURG

Here is a tasty twist to the familiar Waldorf salad. Tofu adds texture to this sweet dressing, one that is sure to be used for other salads, both vegetable and fruit.

5   Red Delicious apples, sliced
¼   cup fresh lemon juice
1   cup water
3   stalks celery, diced
1   (8-ounce) can pineapple tidbits in unsweetened pineapple juice, drained
⅓   cup walnuts, coarsely chopped
❧   *garnish:* mint sprigs

Dressing:
1   cup plain low-fat yogurt
½   cup tofu
1   tablespoon honey
1   teaspoon ground cinnamon

Place sliced apples in mixture of lemon juice and water. Add more water if needed to cover apples.

At serving time, drain liquid from apples. Combine apples, celery, pineapple, and nuts.

For the dressing: Combine yogurt, tofu, honey, and cinnamon in a food processor and blend until smooth. Chill.

Combine apple mixture with dressing and toss gently. Garnish with mint sprigs.

Serves 8
Per ½ cup serving: 119 calories, 4 grams protein, 19 grams carbohydrate, 4 grams fat (29%), 2 milligrams cholesterol, 30 milligrams sodium.

THREE-BEAN SALAD
WITH ARTICHOKE HEARTS

The marinated artichoke hearts add pizazz to this familiar dish. The colors are unique and the nutrition is impressive.

½   pound fresh green beans, steamed or microwaved just until tender
1   (8-ounce) can kidney beans, drained and rinsed
1   (8-ounce) can garbanzo beans, drained and rinsed
2   medium carrots, scrubbed and sliced
2   large celery stalks, thinly sliced
1   medium onion, diced
¼   cup fresh parsley, chopped
1   tablespoon fresh dill, snipped, or ½ teaspoon dried dill weed
½   cup part-skim mozzarella cheese, cubed
1   (4.4-ounce) jar marinated artichoke hearts, drained, marinade reserved romaine lettuce leaves
1   medium tomato, cut into wedges
¼   cup lemon juice
1   teaspoon dried basil leaves
❧   *garnish:* fresh parsley

Combine green beans, kidney beans, garbanzo beans, carrots, celery, onion, parsley, dill, and mozzarella in a large bowl.

When ready to serve, add artichoke hearts. Toss lightly. Line a large, shallow bowl or deep platter with romaine leaves. Spoon bean salad onto leaves. Core and slice tomato; arrange on top of salad.

Mix reserved artichoke marinade, lemon juice, and basil; drizzle over salad. Garnish with chopped parsley.

Serves 8
Per ½ cup serving: 161 calories, 10 grams protein, 21 grams carbohydrate, 5 grams fat (25%), 8 milligrams cholesterol, 286 milligrams sodium.

♣
GRAPE CIDER

*Make sure you stay warm and toasty at the
game by filling your thermos and mugs with
this spicy beverage. Don't forget to bring the
wool blankets, scarves, and mittens, too.*

¼ cup sugar
1 ½ cups water
2 large cinnamon sticks
12 whole cloves
½ cup fresh lemon juice
1 quart unsweetened grape juice

Combine the sugar, water, cinnamon
sticks, and cloves in a large saucepan. Bring
to a boil. Reduce heat to medium and maintain a rolling boil for 10 to 15 minutes.
Remove the cinnamon and cloves.

Add the lemon juice and grape juice.
Simmer for 10 minutes more or until heated
through. Serve warm.

Makes about 6 cups
Per 1 cup serving: 169 calories, 1 gram protein,
42 grams carbohydrate, less than 1 gram fat (1%),
0 milligrams cholesterol, 7 milligrams sodium.

☙
APRICOT-RAISIN BARS

*Sweet, chewy, spicy were a few words our
tasters used to describe this recipe. The added
bonus: iron. The dried fruits supply this often-
neglected mineral.*

Filling:
½ cup dried apricots, diced
¼ cup raisins
½ cup apples, peeled and grated
½ cup reduced-sugar apricot preserves

Crust:
1 ½ teaspoons baking soda
1 cup all-purpose flour
½ cup oat bran
2 cups rolled oats
1 teaspoon ground cinnamon
1 cup brown sugar
¾ cup reduced-calorie margarine, melted

In a medium bowl, combine all filling
ingredients. Stir well.

In a large bowl, combine baking soda,
flour, oat bran, oats, cinnamon, and brown
sugar. Stir in melted margarine. Press slightly
more than half of crust mixture in bottom of
a 9-by-13-inch pan sprayed with vegetable
cooking spray. Spread on filling. Sprinkle
on remaining crust. Bake at 325 degrees for
20 minutes. Cut into bars.

Makes 24 bars
Per 2 inch square: 151 calories, 2 grams protein,
27 grams carbohydrate, 4 grams fat (26%), 0
milligrams cholesterol, 124 milligrams sodium.

CHANGING COLORS

One of the things my son, Parker, looks forward to each autumn is raking leaves. Most kids abhor this task. But Parker enjoys piling colorful leaves as high as he can. Then he jumps right in the middle, burying himself to the neck. Eventually he and I start throwing leaves at each other, and soon we're right back to where we started. Oh, well!

♣
TOMATO-SPINACH-MOZZARELLA SANDWICHES

This quick-to-fix sandwich is full of flavor and color. The red and green of the tomato and the spinach remind me of fall, when the mountains are speckled with orange-red scrub oak and evergreen pines.

½ teaspoon garlic powder
1 teaspoon dried parsley
8 slices French or sourdough bread
16-20 (about ½ pound) spinach leaves, washed and trimmed
4 ounces part-skim mozzarella cheese, thinly sliced
2 medium tomatoes, thinly sliced
2 tablespoons romano cheese, grated

Combine garlic and parsley; sprinkle on bread. Cover each slice with spinach, then top with mozzarella and tomatoes. Place under broiler for 4 to 5 minutes until cheese is melted. Sprinkle with romano cheese. Serve open-faced.

Serves 8
Per serving: 158 calories, 9 grams protein, 21 grams carbohydrate, 4 grams fat (25%), 9 milligrams cholesterol, 321 milligrams sodium.

ᴇ᷍
MARINATED CORN SALAD

Try to use fresh corn cut off the cob for a perky, sweet taste. This salad is even more flavorful the second time around because the seasonings blend with time.

2 cups fresh corn kernels, cooked, or 1 (16-ounce) package frozen corn, cooked and drained
⅔ cup green pepper, chopped
½ cup celery, finely chopped
¼ cup lemon juice
¼ cup vegetable oil
¼ cup sugar
2 green onions (white and green parts), sliced
2 tablespoons fresh parsley, chopped
¼ teaspoon garlic powder

In a medium bowl, combine all ingredients; mix well. Add salt and pepper, if desired, to taste. Cover and chill for at least 8 hours, stirring occasionally to blend flavors.

Serves 6
Per ½ cup serving: 142 calories, 3 grams protein, 26 grams carbohydrate, 5 grams fat (27%), 0 milligrams cholesterol, 10 milligrams sodium.

M·E·N·U

Tomato-Spinach-Mozzarella Sandwiches
•
Marinated Corn Salad
•
Pumpkin & Potato Soup in Acorn Squash
•
Cranberry-Apple Soda
•
Sunny Carrot Cake With Yogurt-Cheese Frosting

PUMPKIN & POTATO SOUP IN ACORN SQUASH

This soup reminds me of the golden-orange color of maple trees during autumn. The flavor is mild, even soothing. The pumpkin and squash, both rich in vitamin A, help to revitalize your skin and hair.

1 tablespoon reduced-calorie margarine
1 small onion, chopped
1 medium russet potato, peeled and diced
1 (16-ounce) can mashed pumpkin
1 tablespoon dried parsley
2 cups Vegetable Broth (see below)
6 acorn squash
¾ cup low-fat milk
¼ cup light cream
❧ *garnish:* green onion and/or celery sticks

In a 5- to 6-quart saucepan, melt margarine over medium heat. Add onion; cook, stirring occasionally, until onion is translucent (about 10 minutes). Stir in potato, pumpkin, parsley, and vegetable broth; bring mixture to a boil; reduce heat to low. Cover and simmer until vegetables are tender when pierced (about 20 minutes). Stir often.

Cut tops off acorn squash and remove seeds. Place in a 9-by-13-inch microwave-safe casserole dish; cover with vented plastic wrap. Microwave squash on HIGH for 8 minutes or until squash is tender. Scoop out squash pulp, leaving a ¼-inch rim on shells. Add to soup mixture; blend well. Reserve squash shells.

Purée soup mixture with an electric mixer until smooth. Stir in milk and cream. Add ¼ teaspoon salt and pepper, if desired, or to taste. Stir on medium-high heat until hot.

Ladle into prepared acorn squash shells. Garnish with green onion and/or celery sticks.

Serves 6
Per serving: 136 calories, 6 grams protein, 22 grams carbohydrate, 3 grams fat (20%), 6 milligrams cholesterol, 358 milligrams sodium.

Vegetable Broth:
4 cups (about 1 pound) carrots, sliced
6 cups (about 2 pounds) celery, without leaves, chopped
2 cups leeks, coarsely chopped
2 cups (about ¼ pound) parsley, chopped
1 ½ cups zucchini, coarsely chopped
1 ½ cups green beans, coarsely chopped
1 cup parsnips, peeled and chopped
1 cup green bell peppers, coarsely chopped
2 bay leaves
2 teaspoons dried marjoram leaves, crushed
1 teaspoon salt
16 cups water

Combine all the ingredients in a large stockpot and bring to a boil. Then reduce heat and simmer, uncovered, for 30 minutes. Remove the pot from the heat and let it sit another 30 minutes.

Strain the stock and discard the vegetables or purée them as a side dish. Refrigerate the stock in a tightly covered container or store in the freezer in the size containers most used for individual recipes. Freeze some in an ice cube tray to use in sautéeing.

Makes about 3 quarts

CRANBERRY-APPLE SODA

The amber of apples and the rich red of cranberries combine to make this a luscious cooler. For a variation, make an ice ring by pouring the soda into a mold and layering slices of lemon and lime. Freeze until solid. Remove by placing bottom of mold in warm water for 1 minute. Add to punch bowl and pour cranberry cocktail and apple juice over ice ring.

4 cups unsweetened cranberry cocktail
4 cups unsweetened apple juice
24 ounces diet lemon-lime soda

Combine cranberry cocktail with apple juice. Chill. When ready to serve, add soda.

Serves 22
Per ½ cup serving: 47 calories, less than 1 gram protein, 12 grams carbohydrate, less than 1 gram fat (less than 1%), 0 milligrams cholesterol, 9 milligrams sodium.

The leaves fall early this autumn, in wind. The paired butterflies are already yellow with August over the grass in the West garden.
—EZRA POUND

♣

Green Pepper Cups Stuffed With Garden Vegetable Pilaf

In the late summer, our gardens swell with green peppers. Full of vitamin C and potassium, this crispy vegetable adds nutrition and color. This is especially true if both the yellow and red varieties are used. Combining the vegetables with grain (rice) and cheese makes this a protein-complete entree.

3 large green peppers, halved lengthwise and seeded
1 cup tofu, drained and finely chopped
¼ cup green onions (white and green parts), sliced
¼ cup celery, chopped
¼ cup carrots, grated
½ cup broccoli, chopped
2 cloves garlic, minced
1 tablespoon reduced-calorie margarine
2 cups cooked brown rice
½ cup cheddar cheese, grated
   seasoned bread crumbs

Arrange green peppers, cut sides up, in a 9-by-13-inch microwave-safe baking dish. Steam for 7 to 10 minutes or microwave on HIGH for 3 minutes. Drain. Set aside.

In a large skillet, cook tofu, green onions, celery, carrots, broccoli, and garlic in margarine until vegetables are crisp-tender. Gently stir in rice and cheese. Add ¼ teaspoon salt and pepper, if desired, or to taste.

Stuff each pepper half with ⅔ cup mixture. Cover and bake at 350 degrees for 25 minutes or microwave on HIGH for 6 minutes. Sprinkle bread crumbs over pepper cups. Bake an additional 5 minutes or until crumbs are golden brown.

Serves 6

Per serving: 191 calories, 9 grams protein, 25 grams carbohydrate, 7 grams fat (31%), 10 milligrams cholesterol, 116 milligrams sodium.

AUTUMN VEGETABLE SOUP

This hearty soup is perfect for the cooler days of autumn. It's a great clean-out-the-refrigerator kind of recipe, so feel free to substitute what you have on hand for any of the suggested vegetables. This freezes well too, so make a double recipe. By the way, I leave the skins on the vegetables when possible to provide maximum fiber. Just be sure to scrub them well.

    2 medium potatoes, cubed
    1 medium onion, coarsely chopped
    2 large carrots, sliced
    3 large stalks celery, sliced
    1 cup green peas, fresh or frozen
    1 cup green beans, fresh or frozen
    1 cup fresh broccoli, chopped
    1 cup corn kernels
    4 cups tomato juice
    3 cups water
    ¼ cup fresh parsley, chopped, or 2 table-
       spoons dried parsley
    1 teaspoon garlic powder
    2 bay leaves
    2 teaspoons dried basil leaves

Combine vegetables, juice, water, and seasonings in a large stockpot. Add salt and pepper, if desired, to taste. Let simmer several hours until vegetables are tender. Remove bay leaves just before serving.

Serves 8
Per 1 cup serving: 120 calories, 5 grams protein, 27 grams carbohydrate, less than 1 gram fat (3%), 0 milligrams cholesterol, 487 milligrams sodium.

APPLE-PEAR CRISP & YOGURT DESSERT SAUCE

At harvest time, I look forward to an abundance of apples and pears. This dessert is a simple and wonderful way to use these autumn fruits. My children savor the sweet smells; I appreciate the fiber boost. I think you'll find the sauce is a versatile substitute for sweet creams.

Fruit:
    4 cups (about 6 apples) tart apples,
       peeled and sliced
    4 cups (about 6 pears) pears, peeled and
       sliced
    2 tablespoons lemon juice
    ¼ cup sugar
    ½ teaspoon ground cinnamon

Topping:
 1 ½ cups quick-cooking rolled oats
    ¼ cup oat bran
    ¼ cup flour
    ½ cup brown sugar
    1 teaspoon ground cinnamon
    ¼ cup reduced-calorie margarine

Yogurt Dessert Sauce:
    ½ cup part-skim ricotta cheese
    ½ cup plain low-fat yogurt
    3 tablespoons sugar
    1 teaspoon vanilla extract

Preheat oven to 350 degrees. Spray a 9-by-13-inch baking dish with vegetable cooking spray.

In a large bowl, combine apples, pears, lemon juice, sugar, and cinnamon. Transfer to prepared pan.

In a medium bowl, combine oats, oat bran, flour, brown sugar, and cinnamon. With pastry blender, cut in margarine until uniformly crumbly. Sprinkle topping over apple mixture. Bake for 45 minutes.

Combine sauce ingredients in food processor or blender; process until satin smooth. Chill until ready to serve. Spoon over warm dessert.

Serves 12
Per serving: 239 calories, 5 grams protein, 39 grams carbohydrate, 7 grams fat (26%), 1 milligram cholesterol, 64 milligrams sodium.

For Papa

My father is a charming man who has friends all over the country because he is a warm, demonstrative, and deeply concerned person. I always have admired his ability to create beautiful art. Food presentations also can represent creative art forms.

M·E·N·U

*Spinach Salad
With
Lime–Poppy Seed
Dressing*

•

*Herbed Parmesan
Tomatoes*

•

*Artichoke-Spinach
Bake*

•

*Oatmeal Cookie
Sandwiches
&
Raisin Sauce*

•

Kay's Almond Drink

♣

Spinach Salad With Lime–Poppy Seed Dressing

I enjoy this recipe for its unique flavor and color combinations, and also for its nutritional value. The vitamin C in the oranges enhances absorption of the iron in the spinach.

1 bunch spinach leaves, washed and trimmed
5-6 green onions (white and green parts), thinly sliced
1 cup bean sprouts, washed and drained well
1 cup mushrooms, scrubbed and sliced
1 (8-ounce) can mandarin oranges, drained
¼ cup slivered almonds, toasted

Dressing:
⅓ cup honey
¼ teaspoon lime peel, finely shredded
3 tablespoons lime juice
1 ½ teaspoons poppy seed
¼ teaspoon salt
⅛ teaspoon ground mace
¼ cup vegetable oil

Combine spinach leaves, onions, sprouts, and mushrooms in a large bowl; toss well. Layer oranges and toasted almonds on top.

For the dressing: In a small bowl, stir together all ingredients except oil. Beat mixture with an electric mixer on medium-high speed while gradually adding salad oil. Continue beating until mixture thickens. Cover; chill. Stir to mix before serving. If, after chilling, mixture becomes too thick, let stand at room temperature for 30 minutes. Makes about ¾ cup.

When ready to serve, drizzle dressing over salad; toss well.

Serves 8
Per serving: 134 calories, 3 grams protein, 20 grams carbohydrate, 6 grams fat (37%), 0 milligrams cholesterol, 116 milligrams sodium.

♣ HERBED PARMESAN TOMATOES

I learned to love tomatoes by watching my father eat fresh whole tomatoes straight from the garden. Broiling tomatoes in this dish preserves their moisture, luscious color, and flavor.

18 (½ inch thick) tomato slices (about 4 medium)
⅓ cup Italian bread crumbs
2 tablespoons Parmesan cheese, grated
¾ teaspoon fresh basil, finely chopped, or ¼ teaspoon dried basil leaves
2 teaspoons fresh parsley, chopped
1 tablespoon reduced-calorie margarine, melted
❧ *garnish:* fresh basil and parsley sprigs

Place tomato slices on a broiler pan sprayed with vegetable cooking spray; set aside.

In a small bowl, combine bread crumbs, Parmesan cheese, basil, parsley, and margarine; mix thoroughly. Sprinkle over tomato slices; broil for 5 minutes until golden brown. Garnish with fresh basil sprigs and parsley sprigs.

Serves 6

Per serving (3 slices): 54 calories, 2 grams protein, 8 grams carbohydrate, 2 grams fat (33%), 2 milligrams cholesterol, 106 milligrams sodium.

♋ ARTICHOKE-SPINACH BAKE

My father loves unusual food combinations, so this is a favorite. Savory artichoke hearts match the subtle taste of spinach in this quiche-like dish. I like the brown rice crust!

Crust:
2 cups cooked brown rice
1 egg white, lightly beaten, or ¼ cup frozen egg substitute, thawed
¼ cup part-skim mozzarella cheese, shredded
¼ teaspoon dried dill weed

Filling:
1 (4.4-ounce) jar marinated artichoke hearts, drained and sliced
1 (10-ounce) package chopped spinach, thawed and drained
¾ cup part-skim mozzarella cheese, shredded
2 egg whites or ½ cup frozen egg substitute, thawed
1 cup low-fat milk
3-4 green onions (white and green parts), thinly sliced
1 teaspoon dried thyme leaves

For the crust: Combine rice, egg white, cheese, and dill weed; stir well. With greased fingers, press mixture into a 9-inch pie plate coated with vegetable cooking spray. Bake at 350 degrees for 5 minutes; set aside.

Arrange artichoke hearts and spinach in the crust. Sprinkle with cheese.

In a small bowl, combine egg whites, milk, green onions, and thyme. Add salt and pepper, if desired, to taste; beat well. Pour over artichoke-spinach mixture. Bake at 350 degrees for 50 minutes or until set. Let stand 5 minutes before serving.

Serves 6

Per ⅙ of pie: 244 calories, 17 grams protein, 24 grams carbohydrate, 9 grams fat (32%), 22 milligrams cholesterol, 396 milligrams sodium.

❧ Garden Vegetable Casserole

The combination of fresh garden vegetables in this dish reminds us to give thanks for a bountiful harvest. My family enjoys this recipe so much that it has become one of the family heirlooms.

   3 cups (about ½ medium head) cauliflower florets
   3 cups (about 6 medium) carrots, sliced diagonally, ½ inch thick
   3 cups (about 1 large bunch) broccoli, cut into 1-inch pieces
   ½ cup reduced-calorie mayonnaise
   ½ cup plain low-fat yogurt
   6 tablespoons prepared horseradish (optional)
5-6 green onions (white and green parts), thinly sliced
   ½ cup fine dry bread crumbs
   2 tablespoons reduced-calorie margarine, melted
   ½ cup sharp cheddar cheese, grated
 ❧ *garnish:* fresh parsley and paprika

In a microwave-safe bowl, microwave cauliflower, carrots, and broccoli on HIGH for 6 to 7 minutes until crisp-tender.

In a small mixing bowl, combine mayonnaise, yogurt, horseradish, and green onions. Add ¼ teaspoon salt and pepper, if desired, or to taste.

Place vegetables in a 2-quart casserole dish. Spread mayonnaise mixture over the vegetables. Sprinkle on bread crumbs; drizzle margarine on top. Bake, covered, in a 350 degree oven for 15 minutes. Remove cover and sprinkle cheese over top; bake an additional 5 minutes until topping is golden and cheese is melted. Garnish with fresh chopped parsley and paprika.

Serves 12

Per serving: 163 calories, 7 grams protein, 17 grams carbohydrate, 9 grams fat (44%), 17 milligrams cholesterol, 243 milligrams sodium.

❧ Dried Fruit & Nut Dressing

This dressing is nutritionally essential for this menu because the grain (bread) combines with the nuts for a protein-complete winner.

   2 tablespoons reduced-calorie margarine
   1 Granny Smith apple, diced
   ½ cup mixed dried fruit, diced
   1 stalk celery, chopped
  10 slices (about 6 cups) whole-wheat bread, cubed
   4 green onions (white and green parts), sliced
   2 tablespoons fresh parsley, chopped
   ¼ teaspoon dried thyme leaves
   ½ cup Vegetable Broth (see p. 91)
   2 tablespoons each of toasted almonds, pine nuts, and sunflower seeds

Microwave Directions:

In a large microwave-safe bowl, melt margarine. Stir in apple, dried fruit, and celery. Cover with plastic wrap and vent one side. Cook on HIGH for 3 minutes. Stir. Cook for another 3 minutes or until soft.

Stir in bread, green onions, parsley, and thyme. Add salt, if desired, to taste. Pour broth over bread mixture and mix gently. Cover with plastic wrap and vent one side. Cook on HIGH for about 5 minutes or until heated through.

When ready to serve, stir in pine nuts, almonds, and sunflower seeds.

Conventional Directions:

In a large saucepan, melt margarine. Add apple, dried fruit, and celery; cook until mixture is soft.

Stir in bread, green onions, parsley, and thyme. Add salt, if desired, to taste. Mix well. Add broth; cook 1 more minute.

Place dressing in a 2-quart baking dish sprayed with vegetable cooking spray. Bake, uncovered, in a 350 degree oven for 15 minutes or until heated through. When ready to serve, stir in pine nuts, almonds, and sunflower seeds.

Serves 6

Per ¾ cup serving: 300 calories, 9 grams protein, 45 grams carbohydrate, 12 grams fat (33%), 0 milligrams cholesterol, 480 milligrams sodium.

TWO-POTATO TWIRLS

Turn two of the family's favorites—sweet potatoes and mashed potatoes—into an eye-pleasing, delicious dish. This is surprisingly quick to prepare.

  3 large baking potatoes
  3 large sweet potatoes or yams or 1 (16-ounce) can cut yams, drained well
  2 tablespoons reduced-calorie margarine, divided
  ½ cup fresh parsley, chopped
  2 tablespoons low-fat milk
  2 tablespoons apricot nectar
  1 tablespoon honey

Peel and quarter potatoes. Place white potatoes and sweet potatoes or yams in separate saucepans. Cook in a small amount of boiling salted water, covered, about 20 minutes or until potatoes are tender. Drain.

Beat hot white potatoes with an electric mixer on low speed until almost smooth. Add 1 tablespoon margarine and milk. Continue beating until light and fluffy. Stir in parsley.

Beat hot sweet potatoes with an electric mixer on low speed until almost smooth. Add remaining margarine, apricot nectar, and honey. Continue beating until light and fluffy.

Spray a baking sheet with vegetable cooking spray. Spoon white potato and sweet potato mixtures into separate decorating bags fitted with large star tips. For twirls: On the prepared baking sheet, pipe 3-inch circles of the sweet potato mixture. Pipe smaller circles of the white potato mixture on top of the sweet potato circles. Make 8 twirls. Cover loosely with plastic wrap; chill until baking time.

Bake, uncovered, in a 375 degree oven for 15 to 20 minutes. The tips should be golden and twirls heated through. Use a wide spatula to transfer the twirls to dinner plates.

Serves 8
Per serving: 135 calories, 2 grams protein, 26 grams carbohydrate, 3 grams fat (19%), less than 1 milligram cholesterol, 43 milligrams sodium.

ALMOND-PUMPKIN MUFFINS WITH STREUSEL TOPPING

Thanksgiving gatherings do not seem complete without pumpkin. This recipe, although not as sweet as pumpkin pie, fills the need nicely. The moist muffin covered by the crumbly Streusel Topping makes a pleasant ending to a delicious meal.

  ⅓ cup reduced-calorie margarine
  1 cup brown sugar
  ⅓ cup light molasses
  2 egg whites
  1 cup pumpkin, mashed
  1 cup oat bran
  1 cup all-purpose flour
  1 tablespoon pumpkin pie spice
  ½ teaspoon baking soda
  ¼ teaspoon baking powder
  ½ cup whole almonds, chopped

Streusel Topping:
  2 tablespoons all-purpose flour
  ¼ cup sugar
  ½ teaspoon ground cinnamon
  1 tablespoon reduced-calorie margarine

In a medium bowl, cream margarine, sugar, and molasses. Add egg whites and pumpkin. Mix well.

In a large bowl, combine oat bran, flour, pumpkin pie spice, baking soda, and baking powder. Add ¼ teaspoon salt, if desired, to taste. Add creamed mixture to flour mixture. Stir just until moistened. Stir in almonds.

For the topping: Combine flour, sugar, and cinnamon. Cut in margarine until mixture is crumbly.

Spoon batter into muffin cups sprayed with vegetable cooking spray, filling ¾ full. Sprinkle topping over batter. Bake in preheated 350 degree oven for 35 to 40 minutes or until wooden pick comes out clean.

Makes 12 muffins
Per muffin: 220 calories, 4 grams protein, 36 grams carbohydrate, 8 grams fat (32%), 0 milligrams cholesterol, 158 milligrams sodium.

CONGRATULATIONS ARE IN ORDER

We have all experienced the personal satisfaction that comes when we accomplish something, whether large or small. This positive reinforcement encourages us to begin again because the secret of success is not necessarily talent, but extraordinary persistence.

M·E·N·U

Tomato Cocktail

•

Mixed
Greens 'N Things
Salad

•

Spinach-Tofu Lasagna

•

Whole-Wheat Scones

•

Three-Apple Topping

•

Texas Chocolate
Sheet Cake
With
Fudge Frosting

TOMATO COCKTAIL

Whatever the cause for congratulations, a toast is in order. A healthful, spicy beverage is just the thing to get the party rolling. This one is best served over ice.

- 1 (46-ounce) can tomato juice
- 1 cup catsup
- ⅓ teaspoon Worcestershire sauce (optional)
- 3 teaspoons sugar
- ½ teaspoon garlic powder
  juice of ½ lemon
- 1 tablespoon horseradish (optional)
- 1 cup celery, finely chopped
- ½ cup fresh parsley, chopped
- *garnish:* celery sticks

Place all ingredients, except garnish, in food processor or electric blender. Process until smooth. Chill several hours or overnight. Serve hot or cold with celery sticks.

Makes about 8 cups
Per 1 cup serving: 75 calories, 2 grams protein, 18 grams carbohydrate, less than 1 gram fat (3%), 0 milligrams cholesterol, 969 milligrams sodium.

MIXED GREENS 'N THINGS SALAD

Very few green salads can be made ahead.

This one, however, will keep up to 24 hours. Preparing this salad ahead allows you time to relax, mingle with your guests, and be the consummate host.

- 4 cups green or red leaf lettuce, torn
- 4 cups iceberg lettuce, torn
- 1 cup celery, thinly sliced
- 2 carrots, peeled and grated
- ½ cup green onion (white and green parts), thinly sliced
- 1 (8-ounce) can water chestnuts, sliced
- 1 (10-ounce) package frozen petite peas

Dressing:
- 1 ½ cups plain low-fat yogurt
- ½ cup reduced-calorie mayonnaise
- 2 teaspoons sugar
- ¼ cup Parmesan cheese, grated
- ¼ teaspoon garlic powder
- *garnish:* imitation bacon bits and tomato wedges

Place lettuce in bottom of shallow salad bowl. Top with celery, carrots, green onions, water chestnuts, and frozen peas.

Combine dressing ingredients; spread evenly over the vegetables. Cover and chill for as long as 24 hours.

When ready to serve, garnish with bacon bits and tomato wedges.

Serves 10
Per serving: 129 calories, 5 grams protein, 15 grams carbohydrate, 6 grams fat (39%), 7 milligrams cholesterol, 117 milligrams sodium.

SPINACH-TOFU LASAGNA

Honor your achiever with this prepare-ahead dish that is sure to satisfy. Full of cheesy filling and aromatic sauce, this recipe does not scrimp on the thing that matters most—taste.

Sauce:
- 1 large onion, chopped
- 3 cloves garlic, minced
- ½ cup mushrooms, sliced
- 1 tablespoon olive oil
- 2 (14 ½-ounce) cans Italian-style stewed tomatoes
- 1 (16-ounce) can Italian tomato sauce
- 1 teaspoon each of dried basil, oregano, and rosemary leaves
- 1 tablespoon dried parsley

Noodles and Spinach:
- 8 ounces lasagna noodles
- 1 pound fresh spinach, lightly steamed and chopped, or 1 (10-ounce) package frozen chopped spinach, thawed and drained

Filling:
- 1 cup chopped tofu
- ½ cup part-skim ricotta cheese
- ¼ cup Parmesan cheese, grated
- ½ cup low-fat cottage cheese

Topping:
- 6 ounces part-skim mozzarella cheese, sliced thin

Sauté onions, garlic, and mushrooms in olive oil. Add tomatoes, sauce, and herbs. Simmer for 15 to 20 minutes.

Cook noodles in unsalted water according to package directions until tender. Drain. Rinse in cold water to prevent sticking.

Mix tofu, ricotta, Parmesan, and cottage cheeses. Blend well. Add salt and pepper, if desired, to taste.

Preheat oven to 350 degrees. Assemble ingredients in a 9-by-13-inch baking dish in the following order: small amount of tomato sauce, cooked noodles, ⅓ of spinach, ⅓ of cheese-tofu mixture, tomato sauce. Repeat, ending with sauce. Place thinly sliced mozzarella cheese on top of casserole and bake for about 40 minutes until bubbly. Let stand 15 minutes before serving.

Serves 8
Per serving: 239 calories, 18 grams protein, 23 grams carbohydrate, 10 grams fat (34%), 28 milligrams cholesterol, 794 milligrams sodium.

♣

WHOLE-WHEAT SCONES

Scones can be made up to 2 weeks in advance. Let cool completely and store, tightly wrapped, in freezer. To serve, wrap in aluminum foil; heat in a 350 degree oven for about 10 minutes or until hot. For a variation, cut into different shapes and sizes. Add fruit-flavored yogurt instead of plain.

- ¾ cup all-purpose flour
- ¾ cup whole-wheat flour
- 1 ½ teaspoons baking powder
- ¼ teaspoon baking soda
- ¼ teaspoon salt
- ¼ cup reduced-calorie margarine, cold
- 1 large egg, lightly beaten
- ¾ cup plain low-fat yogurt

Preheat oven to 400 degrees. Mix flours, baking powder, baking soda, and salt in mixing bowl. Cut in margarine with pastry blender until mixture resembles oatmeal. Add egg and yogurt; mix with fork just until dough comes together.

Turn dough out onto floured surface and knead gently about 8 turns. Roll or pat dough 1 inch thick. Cut out scones, using 1 ½-inch round cutter. Place ½ inch apart on baking sheets sprayed with vegetable cooking spray.

Bake scones until puffed and golden brown, 12 to 15 minutes. Transfer to rack and let cool several minutes.

Cut open scones; serve with warm Apple Topping.

Makes 8 scones
Per serving: 137 calories, 5 grams protein, 19 grams carbohydrate, 5 grams fat (32%), 36 milligrams cholesterol, 160 milligrams sodium.

Life is real! Life is earnest!
—HENRY WADSWORTH LONGFELLOW

THREE-APPLE TOPPING

*Every day, in every
way, I am getting
better and better.*
—EMILE COUÉ

*Like most items on this menu, this recipe can
be prepared ahead of time. You may, however,
choose to simmer the fruit while the guests are
arriving so that your home is full of the sweet,
savory smell of spices. Top breads, cooked
cereals, bagels, crackers, fruits, or vegetables
with this versatile, virtually fat-free sauce.*

  2 Granny Smith apples, peeled and
      quartered
  2 McIntosh apples, peeled and
      quartered
  1 Rome apple, peeled and quartered
  1 cup water
  ½ cup brown sugar
  1 teaspoon ground cinnamon
  ½ teaspoon ground nutmeg
  ¼ teaspoon ground ginger

In a large saucepan, combine all of the
ingredients. Bring to a boil. Cover, reduce
heat, and simmer 1 hour and 15 minutes.
Transfer apple mixture to electric blender or
food processor; blend or process until
smooth.

Return apple mixture to saucepan. Simmer, uncovered, stirring frequently, for
about 1 additional hour. The topping is
ready when the apple mixture is dark
brown and no liquid separates from it.

Makes 3 cups

Per 1 tablespoon: 13 calories, less than 1 gram
protein, 4 grams carbohydrate, less than 1 gram fat
(4%), 0 milligrams cholesterol, less than 1 milligram sodium.

TEXAS CHOCOLATE SHEET CAKE WITH FUDGE FROSTING

*Who can resist this luscious-looking, great-
tasting cake smothered with thick, creamy
fudge? Nobody could, so be glad this recipe
makes 32 servings.*

  ½ cup unsweetened cocoa powder
  ½ cup reduced-calorie margarine
  ¼ cup vegetable oil
1 ½ cups water
  3 cups all-purpose flour
  3 cups sugar
  1 tablespoon baking soda
  1 teaspoon ground cinnamon
  1 teaspoon ground nutmeg
      pinch of salt
1 ½ cups buttermilk
  4 eggs, lightly beaten
  1 tablespoon vanilla extract

Fudge Frosting:
1 ½ cups sugar
  2 tablespoons unsweetened cocoa
      powder
1 ½ tablespoons light corn syrup
  ½ cup evaporated low-fat milk
  4 tablespoons reduced-calorie margarine
  ½ teaspoon vanilla extract

In a medium saucepan, combine cocoa,
margarine, oil, and water. Bring to a boil
over medium-high heat, stirring frequently.
Pour into medium bowl; set aside and let
cool.

In a large bowl, combine flour, sugar,
baking soda, cinnamon, nutmeg, and salt.
Set aside.

Stir buttermilk, eggs, and vanilla into
cooled cocoa mixture until well blended.
Add cocoa mixture to dry ingredients. Stir
until well blended. Transfer batter into a
10-by-15-inch pan sprayed with vegetable
cooking spray. Bake in a 400 degree oven for
30 to 35 minutes or until a wooden pick
inserted in the center comes out clean. Cool
on rack before frosting.

For the frosting: In a small saucepan,
combine sugar, cocoa, corn syrup, and milk.
Cook, without stirring, to soft ball stage
(about 15 minutes). Remove from heat.
Add margarine and vanilla. Beat until creamy
and thick. Pour on cake and allow to cool.

Makes 32 servings

Per serving: 264 calories, 3 grams protein, 50
grams carbohydrate, 6 grams fat (22%), 31 milligrams cholesterol, 150 milligrams sodium.

FIRELIGHT WARMTH

I was raised in sunny California. Cold days in Los Angeles meant wearing a lightweight sweater and socks, if you absolutely had to. Our fireplaces served a decorative function. It wasn't until I moved to Rocky Mountain country that I learned what cold really means. Warming my numb hands by firelight reminds me of the true purpose of fireplaces.

ↄ

HEARTY QUICK OR SLOW STEW

If you don't use your Dutch oven (quick), you can put this together in a crock-pot (slow), and let it simmer all day. Then come in from the cold to this irresistible stew, full of everything (almost) that is nutritious and delicious. I dedicate this stew to great carbohydrate-rich potatoes, beans, and lentils.

1 (32-ounce) can tomato juice
2 (14 ¼-ounce) cans stewed tomatoes, Italian style
2 cups water
2 medium potatoes, unpeeled and chopped
1 (15-ounce) can garbanzo beans, drained
1 (15-ounce) can kidney beans, drained
1 cup lentils, rinsed and drained
1 large onion, chopped
1 cup each of red and green peppers, seeded and diced
1 (10-ounce) package frozen chopped spinach
2 carrots, cut into 1-inch julienne strips
2 tablespoons dried parsley
2 tablespoons chili powder (optional)
2 teaspoons dried basil leaves, crushed
2 teaspoons garlic powder
1 teaspoon ground cumin

Topping:
½ cup reduced-calorie sour cream
½ cup plain low-fat yogurt
❧ *garnish:* chives

In a 4 ½-quart Dutch oven, combine all ingredients except sour cream, yogurt, and chives. After bringing mixture to a boil, reduce heat and simmer, covered, about 30 minutes or until lentils are tender.

Garnish each serving with sour cream blended with yogurt and top with snipped chives. Serve with Crispy Tortilla Chips.

Serves 12
Per 1 ½ cup serving: 231 calories, 13 grams protein, 42 grams carbohydrate, 3 grams fat (11%), 3 milligrams cholesterol, 562 milligrams sodium.

♣

CRISPY TORTILLA CHIPS

You save a bundle of fat by making your own chips at home. Make several batches; store the chips in airtight containers for later use.

12 small corn tortillas, cut in 8 wedges
seasoned salt (optional)

Spread tortilla triangles on baking sheet. Sprinkle with seasoned salt, if desired. Then spray tortillas with vegetable cooking spray.

Bake in preheated 500 degree oven for 5 to 10 minutes until golden brown. Allow to cool.

Makes 8 dozen
Per 12 chips: 98 calories, 3 grams protein, 20 grams carbohydrate, 2 grams fat (13%), 0 milligrams cholesterol, 268 milligrams sodium.

M · E · N · U

*Hearty
Quick or Slow Stew*
•
Crispy Tortilla Chips
•
*Winter Greens Salad
&
Watercress Dressing*
•
Dill Bread
•
*Couscous Pudding
With
Raspberry Sauce*
•
Minty Cocoa

Winter Greens Salad & Watercress Dressing

I warm'd both hands before the fire of life.
—WALTER SAVAGE LANDOR

This salad reminds me of a Caesar Salad modified to limit fat. Enjoy the unique flavors of the Watercress Dressing.

2 cups (about ½ small head) curly endive, torn
2 cups (about ½ small head) romaine lettuce, torn
2 cups (about ½ small head) iceberg lettuce, torn
1 medium cucumber, sliced
4-6 green onions (white and green parts), sliced
1 large tomato, cut into wedges
¼ cup seasoned bread crumbs

Watercress Dressing:
½ cup watercress, packed and chopped (no stems)
¼ cup olive oil
2 tablespoons lemon juice
½ teaspoon dried tarragon leaves
1 tablespoon Parmesan cheese, grated
1 clove garlic, minced

For the salad: Combine greens, cucumber, green onions, and tomato. Toss gently.

For the dressing: Combine watercress, oil, lemon juice, tarragon, Parmesan cheese, and garlic. Add salt and pepper, if desired, to taste. Stir well. Pour over salad; toss gently. Sprinkle bread crumbs over salad. Serve immediately.

Serves 6
Per serving: 113 calories, 4 grams protein, 15 grams carbohydrate, 6 grams fat (42%), less than 1 milligram cholesterol, 136 milligrams sodium.

Dill Bread

It takes very few steps to achieve this delicious yeast-raised herb bread. It freezes well, too. The dill complements the soothing flavors in the stew.

1 cup whole-wheat flour
¼ cup sugar
2 teaspoons instant onion, minced
1 ½ tablespoons whole dill seed
2 teaspoons salt
½ teaspoon baking soda
2 packages dry yeast
2 cups low-fat cottage cheese
½ cup water
2 tablespoons reduced-calorie margarine
2 egg whites
4 cups all-purpose flour

In a large bowl, combine whole-wheat flour, sugar, onion, dill seed, salt, baking soda, and yeast.

In a small saucepan, heat cottage cheese, water, and margarine. When very warm, add to dry ingredients. Add egg whites and beat at low speed until dry ingredients are moist. Then beat at medium speed for 3 minutes.

Add enough flour to make a stiff dough. Turn out on a floured surface and knead about 8 times. Place in a warm bowl sprayed with vegetable cooking spray. Cover and let rise in warm place until double (about 1 hour).

Work dough down with spoon and then form into three loaves. Place in bread pans (4 ½-by-8 ½-inches each) sprayed with vegetable cooking spray. Cover and let rise until double (30 to 45 minutes).

Preheat oven to 350 degrees. Bake loaves for about 40 minutes or until brown. Remove from pans and let cool on racks, top side up.

Makes 3 loaves
Per slice: 84 calories, 4 grams protein, 15 grams carbohydrate, less than 1 gram fat (9%), 1 milligram cholesterol, 189 milligrams sodium.

COUSCOUS PUDDING WITH RASPBERRY SAUCE

Although traditionally made with rice, this recipe uses a Middle Eastern ingredient, couscous. It is not actually a grain, but a pasta made from flour-coated semolina.

    4 cups water
    2 cups couscous, uncooked
    2 tablespoons reduced-calorie margarine
    2 cups low-fat milk
    1 cup low-fat evaporated milk
    2 large eggs
    ½ cup sugar
    2 teaspoons vanilla extract
    ½ teaspoon lemon rind, grated
    ⅛ teaspoon ground nutmeg

Raspberry Sauce:
    1 (12-ounce) package frozen unsweetened raspberries, thawed
    ¼ cup reduced-calorie raspberry spread
    1 teaspoon vanilla extract
    ½ teaspoon ground cinnamon

In a medium saucepan, bring the water to a boil; stir in the couscous. Reduce the heat; cover the pan. Simmer the couscous until the water is absorbed (less than 5 minutes). Transfer the couscous to a large bowl; stir in the margarine until it melts and is well distributed.

In a medium bowl, beat together the milks, eggs, sugar, vanilla, lemon rind, and nutmeg. Add this to the couscous; stir the ingredients well.

Transfer the mixture to a 3-quart baking dish sprayed with vegetable cooking spray. Bake the pudding in a 325 degree oven for about 45 minutes or until the pudding is set. Serve the pudding warm or at room temperature with Raspberry Sauce.

For the sauce: Combine all ingredients in medium saucepan over medium-high heat; cook 6 to 8 minutes, stirring occasionally, until bubbly. Refrigerate until ready to serve.

Makes 8 servings
Per serving: 223 calories, 7 grams protein, 44 grams carbohydrate, 3 grams fat (10%), 4 milligrams cholesterol, 104 milligrams sodium.

MINTY COCOA

Nothing takes the chill off a winter day better than a piping hot drink. Welcome home tired sledders and skiers with this minty cocoa, flavored with peppermint candies.

    ¼ cup unsweetened cocoa
    3 tablespoons sugar
    6 starlight candies (red-and-white-striped peppermint candies), finely crushed
    6 cups low-fat milk, divided
    ¼ cup nondairy whipped topping

Combine cocoa, sugar, and crushed candies in a heavy saucepan; stir well.

Add 1 cup milk, stirring well. Gradually add remaining 5 cups milk, stirring well. Cook over medium heat until mixture is thoroughly heated (about 5 minutes), stirring frequently. Top each serving with 1 tablespoon whipped topping.

Serves 4
Per 1 cup serving: 182 calories, 9 grams protein, 30 grams carbohydrate, 4 grams fat (19%), 10 milligrams cholesterol, 127 milligrams sodium.

The fog comes on little cat feet.
—CARL SANDBURG

UNEXPECTED GUESTS

Surprises and spontaneity make life exciting. Handling these unexpected moments with poise and polish is the key. That is why all the recipes in this menu can be prepared within 30 minutes. This gives the cook time to relax and enjoy the unexpected guests.

M·E·N·U

*Basil Pesto Dip
With Crackers*

•

*Pineapple-Banana
Slush*

•

*Marinated Avocado
Salad*

•

Vegetable Stroganoff

•

*Store-and-Bake Bran
Muffins*

♣

BASIL PESTO DIP WITH CRACKERS

Most of us find it easy to make pesto in a blender or food processor. Update the familiar pesto by substituting cilantro, mint, sage, parsley, or sun-dried tomatoes for the basil. Have slices of fresh vegetables on hand to serve along with the crackers.

- ⅓ cup pesto, homemade or purchased
- 8 ounces ricotta cheese, at room temperature
- ¼ cup slivered almonds, toasted

Pesto:
- 3 cloves garlic, minced
- ½ cup fresh basil leaves, firmly packed
- 2 tablespoons blanched almonds
- 2 tablespoons olive oil
- ½ cup Parmesan cheese, grated

For the homemade pesto: Place the garlic, basil, and blanched almonds in the bowl of a food processor or blender. With the motor running, slowly drizzle in the oil through the feed tube; process until the basil is puréed. Transfer the pesto to a bowl and stir in the Parmesan cheese. Add salt and pepper, if desired, to taste. Refrigerate, covered, until ready to use. (Keeps in the refrigerator for 2 to 3 days.) Makes about ⅔ cup.

With a mixer or food processor, beat ricotta and ⅓ cup pesto until well blended. Cover and chill until ready to use.

To serve: Mound cheese mixture on a plate. Sprinkle with slivered almonds. Serve with low-fat whole-grain crackers.

Makes about 1 ½ cups

Per 2 tablespoons pesto dip and 6 crackers: 214 calories, 8 grams protein, 24 grams carbohydrate, 9 grams fat (38%), 15 milligrams cholesterol, 133 milligrams sodium.

♣ PINEAPPLE-BANANA SLUSH

Like all the recipes in this menu, this refreshing tropical blend is a snap to whip up.

- 1 (20-ounce) can pineapple chunks in unsweetened juice
- 1 banana, cut into chunks
- 1 ½ cups low-fat milk
- ½ teaspoon vanilla extract
- 6 ice cubes
- ❦ *garnish:* slices of lime

Drain pineapple, reserving ¾ cup juice. Combine reserved juice and all other ingredients in a blender and process until smooth. Pour into glasses; garnish with slice of lime.

Serves 4
Per 1 cup serving: 138 calories, 4 grams protein, 30 grams carbohydrate, 1 gram fat (8%), 4 milligrams cholesterol, 48 milligrams sodium.

♣ MARINATED AVOCADO SALAD

When the guests arrive, prepare the marinade and cover the oranges, avocado, and onion to allow the flavors to blend.

- ¼ cup orange juice
- 2 tablespoons lemon juice
- 2 teaspoons olive oil
- 1 ½ teaspoons sugar
- 3 oranges, peeled and sectioned
- 1 avocado, peeled and sliced
- 1 small red onion, thinly sliced
- 1 head butter lettuce

In a large bowl, combine juices, olive oil, and sugar. Add ½ teaspoon salt, if desired. Stir in oranges, avocado, and onion. Cover and refrigerate while flavors blend.

Tear lettuce into bite-size pieces. Store sealed and refrigerated until ready to serve.

To serve: Combine mixtures. Gently toss to mix well.

Serves 8
Per serving: 112 calories, 2 grams protein, 17 grams carbohydrate, 5 grams fat (38%), 0 milligrams cholesterol, 139 milligrams sodium.

♣ VEGETABLE STROGANOFF

Many people do not realize that pasta is a low-fat, energy-rich complex carbohydrate. Typically only the creamy, calorie-laden sauces make pasta a forbidden food. This recipe breaks all the rules by combining a rich "creamy" sauce with fiber-filled vegetables and noodles. Enjoy!

- ¾ cup light cream
- ½ cup plain low-fat yogurt
- 1 cup carrots, sliced
- 1 cup broccoli florets
- 1 cup cauliflower florets
- ¾ pound flat noodles
- 1 onion, finely chopped
- ½ pound mushrooms, diced
- 1 tablespoon olive oil
- 3 cloves garlic, crushed
- 3 dashes Worcestershire sauce (optional)
- ❦ *garnish:* dried parsley, dried tarragon leaves, and Parmesan cheese, grated

Blend cream and yogurt until smooth. Set aside. Microwave vegetables in a microwave-safe bowl on HIGH for 5 to 6 minutes until cooked through. Cook noodles until tender; drain. Keep vegetables and noodles warm by placing in a 200 degree oven in a covered dish.

Sauté onion and mushrooms in oil until onion turns translucent. Add garlic; cook for another 3 minutes. Stir in Worcestershire sauce. Add ¼ teaspoon salt and pepper, if desired, or to taste. Reduce heat to low.

When ready to serve, stir cream-yogurt mixture into sautéed mixture to make sauce; heat through. Toss vegetables with noodles; place on serving platter; spoon sauce over top. Garnish with mixture of parsley, tarragon, and Parmesan cheese.

Serves 6
Per serving: 183 calories, 7 grams protein, 24 grams carbohydrate, 7 grams fat (34%), 30 milligrams cholesterol, 49 milligrams sodium.

Conversation is but carving!
Give no more to every guest
Than he's able to digest.
—JONATHAN SWIFT

♣

Store-and-Bake Bran Muffins

Our food stylist, Rebecca Robison, is a busy mother of four children. She shared this time-saving mix, which I have come to count on. Your guests will appreciate freshly baked muffins in the morning, and you hardly will have lifted a finger. I enjoy the whole-grain texture.

  3 cups whole-bran cereal
  1 cup boiling water
  2 cups buttermilk
  ½ cup reduced-calorie margarine
  ½ cup sugar
  2 egg whites
  2 cups all-purpose flour
  1 cup whole-wheat flour
2 ½ teaspoons baking soda
  ½ teaspoon salt, if desired
  ½ cup chopped dried fruit (optional)

In a medium bowl, mix the bran cereal and the boiling water. Set aside. When cool, stir in the buttermilk.

In a large mixing bowl, beat the margarine and the sugar together until creamy. Add the egg whites and blend well. Then stir in the bran-buttermilk mixture.

Combine the all-purpose and whole-wheat flours, baking soda, and salt; add to the bran mixture. Stir just enough to moisten the dry ingredients. Add the dried fruit, if desired.

Divide the batter between 36 small muffin cups or 24 large muffin cups sprayed with vegetable cooking spray, filling each cup about ¾ full. (Or, refrigerate the batter in a tightly closed container for future use. Will keep for up to 3 weeks.)

Bake in a preheated 400 degree oven for 15 to 18 minutes. Remove muffins; let cool on wire rack.

Makes 3 dozen small muffins

Per small muffin: 84 calories, 3 grams protein, 17 grams carbohydrate, 2 grams fat (18%), less than 1 milligram cholesterol, 166 milligrams sodium.

COCOONING

Our fast-paced lifestyles make cocooning more popular. To me, cocooning means settling in with my family for a quiet weekend meal that we all cook together. This gives us time to renew our senses of sound, smell, sight, and taste without the interruptions of busy weekdays.

♣ SWEET POTATO PANCAKES

The nontraditional use of sweet potatoes in this recipe works well. I think you'll enjoy the unusual combinations because the banana enhances the flavor of the sweet potato. Both add big nutritional bonuses, namely potassium and vitamin A. Serve with warm maple syrup. For variations, serve with Citrus Medley With Apricot-Lemon Sauce (see p. 128), Three-Apple Topping (see p. 114), or Spiced Fruit Compote (see p. 103).

1 ¼ cups whole-wheat flour
1 cup rolled oats
¼ cup wheat bran
2 tablespoons sunflower seeds
1 tablespoon baking powder
1 tablespoon sugar
¼ teaspoon baking soda
¼ teaspoon salt
¼ teaspoon ground cinnamon
⅛ teaspoon ground cloves
⅛ teaspoon ground nutmeg
1 cup sweet potato, baked, peeled, and mashed, or ½ (16-ounce) can yams, mashed
1 cup low-fat milk
½ cup plain low-fat yogurt
1 whole egg
1 egg white
1 tablespoon vegetable oil
1 banana, peeled and mashed

In a large bowl, combine the flour, oats, bran, sunflower seeds, baking powder, sugar, baking soda, salt, and spices.

In a medium bowl, whisk together the sweet potato, milk, yogurt, egg, egg white, and oil. Stir in the banana. Combine well.

Add sweet potato mixture to flour mixture, stirring them just to blend. Add more milk if the batter is too thick.

Spray griddle or skillet with vegetable cooking spray. For each pancake, place about 3 tablespoons batter on prepared griddle or skillet. Flip the pancakes when the tops begin to bubble and the undersides are golden brown.

Makes 12 pancakes

Per 1 pancake: 138 calories, 5 grams protein, 23 grams carbohydrate, 3 grams fat (21%), 23 milligrams cholesterol, 172 milligrams sodium.

M·E·N·U

Sweet Potato Pancakes
•
Cheese & Egg Puff
•
Orange Cider
•
*Citrus Medley
With
Apricot-Lemon Sauce*
•
Date Filled Ring

CHEESE & EGG PUFF

This recipe reminds me of a cross between a soufflé and a quiche. The texture is light and fluffy, a perfect companion to the heavier pancake.

2 cups low-fat cottage cheese
½ cup part-skim mozzarella cheese, grated
½ cup Monterey Jack cheese, grated
3 eggs, lightly beaten
3 egg whites, lightly beaten
⅛ teaspoon salt
1 teaspoon baking powder
¼ cup flour
2 tablespoons reduced-calorie margarine, melted
1 (4-ounce) can diced green chiles (optional)
½ cup mushrooms, sliced
½ cup onions, chopped

In a food processor or electric blender, place cheeses, eggs, egg whites, salt, baking powder, flour, and margarine. Process until smooth.

Stir in chiles, mushrooms, and onions. Pour into an 8-inch square pan sprayed with vegetable cooking spray. Bake in a 350 degree oven for 45 to 60 minutes. Cut in squares. Serve hot or cold.

Serves 6

Per serving: 263 calories, 26 grams protein, 11 grams carbohydrate, 12 grams fat (42%), 118 milligrams cholesterol, 724 milligrams sodium.

ORANGE CIDER

Herbal teas are soothing whenever you drink them—at sunrise or just before bedtime. When combined with juices, herbal teas add flavor interest, especially if you choose a spiced variety.

4 cups water
4 cups unsweetened apple cider
2 tablespoons brown sugar
8 whole cloves
2 sticks cinnamon
5 orange and spice herb tea bags

In a large saucepan, combine water, cider, brown sugar, cloves, and cinnamon. Simmer on medium-low heat until heated through and flavors blend. Remove from heat; add orange and spice herb tea bags. Cover and let stand 5 minutes. Remove tea bags, cloves, and cinnamon. Serve warm.

Makes 8 cups

Per 1 cup serving: 69 calories, less than 1 gram protein, 17 grams carbohydrate, less than 1 gram fat (2%), 0 milligrams cholesterol, 13 milligrams sodium.

Dost thou love life? Then do not squander time, for that is the stuff life is made of.
—BENJAMIN FRANKLIN

❧ Citrus Medley with Apricot-Lemon Sauce

The winter season is the best time for beautiful citrus fruit. Select firm and heavy fruits with smooth and unblemished skins. Combine varieties for endless ways to flavor and enhance dishes.

1 medium orange, peeled, seeded, and sectioned
1 grapefruit, peeled, seeded, and sectioned
1 tangerine, peeled, seeded, and sectioned
1 tangelo, peeled, seeded, and sectioned
1 (11-ounce) can mandarin oranges, drained
4 kumquats, unpeeled and thinly sliced.

Apricot-Lemon Sauce:
1 tablespoon brown sugar
⅛ teaspoon ground mace
½ cup lemon low-fat yogurt
¼ cup apricot nectar
❧ *garnish:* lemon slices and fresh mint sprigs.

Divide and arrange fruit on 6 plates.

For the Apricot-Lemon Sauce: Stir brown sugar and mace into the lemon yogurt. Add apricot nectar. Stir until smooth. (May be stored in the refrigerator for up to 2 weeks.)

Drizzle dressing over fruit. Garnish with lemon slices and fresh mint sprigs.

Serves 6

Per serving: 120 calories, 2 grams protein, 30 grams carbohydrate, less than 1 gram fat (3%), less than 1 milligram cholesterol, 18 milligrams sodium.

❧ Date-Filled Ring

This low-fat adaptation of traditional coffee cake is mouthwatering. I appreciate how quickly it can be prepared.

1 ½ cups buttermilk baking mix
½ cup whole-wheat flour
2 tablespoons sugar
3 tablespoons reduced-calorie margarine, melted
½ cup low-fat milk
2 egg whites, slightly beaten
Date Filling (see below)
¼ cup honey

Date Filling:
½ cup dates, chopped*
½ cup brown sugar, packed
¼ cup reduced-calorie margarine, melted
1 teaspoon ground cinnamon
¼ cup walnuts, chopped

In a large bowl, combine baking mix, flour, sugar, margarine, milk, and egg whites until dough forms; then beat for 30 seconds. Spread half of dough into an 8-inch round cake pan sprayed with vegetable cooking spray.

For the Date Filling: In a medium bowl, combine dates, sugar, margarine, cinnamon, and walnuts. Spread over dough in pan. Then cover with remaining dough.

Bake at 350 degrees about 35 minutes. Cool 10 minutes on a wire rack. Drizzle honey over top, cut in wedges, and serve warm.

Serves 8

Per serving: 316 calories, 5 grams protein, 58 grams carbohydrate, 8 grams fat (22%), less than 1 milligram cholesterol, 425 milligrams sodium.

*If you do not purchase chopped dates, chill whole dates and then cut them into small pieces with kitchen scissors.

WINTER WORKOUTS

My father was convinced that a family that skis together stays together, so I learned to snow ski at a young age. Keeping up with my brothers and my husband, Michael, helps me stay fit during the winter months. Skiing, along with many other vigorous winter sports, stimulates our appetites. Satisfy them with the following eye-appealing and healthful recipes.

M·E·N·U

*Cream of
Potato & Watercress
Soup*

•

*Parmesan Breadstick
Twists*

•

*Fresh Fruit & Blue
Cheese Salad*

•

*Sweet
Onion & Blended
Cheese Pizza*

•

Apricot Refresher

•

Banana Snack Cake

♣

CREAM OF POTATO & WATERCRESS SOUP

When muscles ache, you may need to replace potassium, and you'll find plenty of it in potatoes and watercress. This soup is an unforgettable flavor experience. Simply delicious!

2 tablespoons reduced-calorie margarine
1 small onion, chopped
1 cup leeks (white part and 1-inch green), thinly sliced
1 pound (about 3 medium) potatoes, peeled and diced
3 cups Vegetable Broth (see p. 91)
1 ½ teaspoons dried tarragon leaves
1 ½ teaspoons dried thyme leaves
1 cup watercress, packed (no stems)
1 cup low-fat milk
1 cup evaporated low-fat milk

In a large saucepan, melt the margarine; sauté the onion and leeks until translucent (about 10 minutes). Add the potatoes and broth. Bring to a boil. Reduce the heat, partially cover the pan, and simmer the soup until the vegetables are tender (about 10 minutes). Season with the tarragon and thyme. Add half the watercress; simmer for 1 minute more.

Transfer the soup to a blender or food processor; purée. Return the purée to the saucepan.

Heat over a moderately low flame and add the remaining watercress and milks; heat through, stirring well, but do not boil. Adjust the seasonings with salt and pepper, if desired, and serve.

Serves 6
Per 1 ½ cup serving: 184 calories, 9 grams protein, 26 grams carbohydrate, 5 grams fat (25%), 4 milligrams cholesterol, 513 milligrams sodium, 646 milligrams potassium.

♣

PARMESAN BREADSTICK TWISTS

These are quick to prepare and a fun "twist" to the traditional garlic bread. Slice leftover breadsticks and allow to dry for delicious croutons in salads or soups.

1 package whole-grain ready-made breadsticks
¼ cup reduced-calorie margarine, melted
1 teaspoon garlic powder
¼ cup Parmesan cheese, grated
   cornmeal

Uncoil breadsticks. Combine margarine and garlic powder. Dip breadsticks in margarine mixture; then roll in Parmesan cheese. Twist. Place on a baking sheet that has been sprinkled with cornmeal. Bake at 375 degrees for 12 to 15 minutes.

Makes 8 breadsticks
Per breadstick: 69 calories, 2 grams protein, 8 grams carbohydrate, 3 grams fat (37%), 2 milligrams cholesterol, 137 milligrams sodium.

Fresh Fruit & Blue Cheese Salad

Challenged muscles need an adequate supply of iron-rich foods. And, the addition of vitamin C–rich foods serves to enhance its absorption. This salad provides a perfect example: iron-rich dark greens with vitamin C–rich citrus.

- 2 cups red leaf lettuce, torn
- 2 cups romaine lettuce, torn
- 2 cups fresh parsley, trimmed
  Grapefruit Dressing (see below)
- 1 ½ cups grapefruit sections, drained
- 1 fresh pear, cored, and cubed in 1-inch pieces
- 2 tablespoons blue cheese, crumbled
  poppy seeds

Combine lettuce and parsley in a large bowl. Add 6 tablespoons Grapefruit Dressing; reserve remaining dressing for another use. Toss lettuce and divide it evenly among 6 salad plates. Top each with grapefruit sections and cubes of pear; sprinkle with blue cheese and poppy seeds. Serve immediately.

Serves 6

Grapefruit Dressing:
- ½ cup unsweetened grapefruit juice
- ¼ cup water
- 1 (0.8-ounce) envelope reduced-calorie Italian salad dressing mix
- 1 tablespoon vegetable oil

Combine grapefruit juice, water, and salad dressing mix in a jar; cover and shake to mix. Add oil; cover and shake again. Chill.

Makes ¾ cup

Per 1 cup salad with 1 tablespoon dressing: 107 calories, 3 grams protein, 19 grams carbohydrate, 2 grams fat (19%), 4 milligrams cholesterol, 150 milligrams sodium, 124% of RDA for vitamin C, 12% of RDA for iron (women's value).

Sweet Onion & Blended Cheese Pizza

This New York–style pizza is easy to prepare and full of calcium-rich ricotta and Parmesan cheeses. Try topping thawed and rolled French bread dough, bagels, English muffins, or pita bread for a crust variation.

- 1 tablespoon reduced-calorie margarine
- 2 large Spanish onions, thinly sliced
- 1 tablespoon sugar
- 1 (10-ounce) package prepared pizza crust
- 1 (15-ounce) container part-skim ricotta cheese
- ⅓ cup Parmesan cheese, grated
- ½ cup part-skim mozzarella cheese, shredded
- 1 ounce sun-dried tomatoes, drained if oil-packed
- ¼ cup fresh parsley, chopped

Preheat oven to 450 degrees. Melt margarine in large skillet. Add onions and sugar. Sauté for 10 to 15 minutes on high, stirring frequently, until onions are caramelized. Keep warm.

While onions are sautéing, unroll pizza crust on a baking sheet sprayed with vegetable cooking spray. Flatten dough into a 10-by-15-inch rectangle. Combine ricotta and Parmesan cheeses. Sprinkle mozzarella over dough; cover with ricotta mixture. Bake on bottom rack of oven until crust is browned (about 10 to 15 minutes). Top with onions, sun-dried tomatoes, and parsley.

Serves 6

Per serving: 314 calories, 18 grams protein, 36 grams carbohydrate, 11 grams fat (31%), 30 milligrams cholesterol, 500 milligrams sodium, 394 milligrams calcium.

People don't notice whether it's winter or summer when they're happy.
—ANTON CHEKHOV

❧ APRICOT REFRESHER

Skiing, sledding, snowmobiling, and other winter-weather challenges demand high-energy food replacements. For instant refreshment—with the added bonus of generous amounts of potassium and vitamin A—take a bottle of this drink with you.

- 1 (14-ounce) can apricot halves in extra-light syrup
- 2 bananas, peeled
- 1 (12-ounce) can apricot nectar
- 1 (8-ounce) cup plain low-fat yogurt
- 1 tablespoon honey
- 1 tablespoon lemon juice
  crushed ice

Purée ingredients in blender until smooth and frothy. Chill briefly and serve over crushed ice.

Serves 5

Per 1 cup serving: 173 calories, 4 grams protein, 40 grams carbohydrate, 1 gram fat (5%), 3 milligrams cholesterol, 38 milligrams sodium, 399 milligrams potassium, 33% of RDA for vitamin A.

☙ BANANA SNACK CAKE

My family would be thrilled to have me bake this cake every day. It is a simple recipe with a subtle taste and light texture.

- 1 ¼ cups all-purpose flour
- 1 cup whole-wheat flour
- 2 teaspoons baking powder
- 1 teaspoon baking soda
- ⅔ cup reduced-calorie margarine, softened
- 1 cup sugar
- ¾ cup egg substitute or 3 egg whites, beaten
- 1 ¼ cups (about 2 large) bananas, mashed
- ⅔ cup plain low-fat yogurt
- ½ cup walnuts, chopped
  confectioners' sugar

Combine flours, baking powder, and baking soda.

In another bowl, cream margarine and sugar at medium speed. At low speed, blend in egg substitute or egg whites and bananas. Add flour mixture alternately with yogurt. Mix until smooth. Stir in walnuts.

Transfer batter into a 9-by-13-inch baking pan sprayed with vegetable cooking spray. Bake at 350 degrees for 45 minutes or until wooden pick inserted in center comes out clean. Cool in pan on wire rack. Dust with confectioners' sugar before serving.

Serves 24

Per serving: 133 calories, 3 grams protein, 21 grams carbohydrate, 5 grams fat (32%), less than 1 milligram cholesterol, 112 milligrams sodium.

HOME FOR THE HOLIDAYS

M·E·N·U

Orange-Peach Frost

•

Holiday Cranberry Salad

•

Festive Broccoli-Topped Holiday Rice

•

Cinnamon-Apple Bread With Yogurt-Cheese Spread

•

Elegant Stuffed Potatoes

•

Minty Chocolate Mousse

ORANGE-PEACH FROST

The tartness of orange blends beautifully with the sweetness of peach here. For a variation, make an ice ring by pouring additional peach juice into a mold; freeze. When you are ready to serve, turn out the ring into a punch bowl.

- 2 cups unsweetened orange juice
- 2 cups frozen peach slices
- ¼ cup peach juice
- 1 cup low-fat milk
- 2 tablespoons sugar
- 1 teaspoon vanilla extract
- ¼ teaspoon ground nutmeg

Combine all ingredients except nutmeg in an electric blender; process mixture until smooth. Pour into glasses. Sprinkle nutmeg on top. Serve immediately over crushed ice.

Serves 5

Per 1 cup serving: 180 calories, 2 grams protein, 44 grams carbohydrate, less than 1 gram fat (2%), 1 milligram cholesterol, 26 milligrams sodium.

HOLIDAY CRANBERRY SALAD

I really like this recipe. The holiday colors make it a visual feast; the sweet cranberries and tart grapes make it a palate pleaser.

- 1 (12-ounce) package fresh or frozen cranberries
- 1 cup sugar
- ½ pound seedless red grapes, halved
- ½ pound seedless green grapes, halved
- 2 large Red Delicious apples, cored and cubed
- 2 large kiwi fruit, sliced
- ½ cup pecans, chopped
- ½ cup nondairy whipped topping
- ½ cup apple-spice low-fat yogurt

Coarsely chop cranberries in a food processor. Transfer cranberries to a bowl. Add sugar. Cover and chill 8 hours.

Drain cranberries for 2 hours, reserving liquid for other uses (see p. 91). Combine cranberries, grapes, apples, kiwi fruit, and pecans.

Combine whipped topping with yogurt. Spoon over fruit and pecans. Chill until ready to serve.

Serves 8

Per 1 cup serving: 273 calories, 2 grams protein, 55 grams carbohydrate, 7 grams fat (22%), less than 1 milligram cholesterol, 13 milligrams sodium.

♣
FESTIVE BROCCOLI-TOPPED HOLIDAY RICE

The sweetness of brown rice and crispy vegetables contrasts nicely with the unexpected crunch of peanuts in this dish. To save time and to enhance blending of flavors, prepare the rice-vegetable mixture in advance.

    1   cup instant brown rice
    2   cups Vegetable Broth (see p. 91)
    2   tablespoons olive oil
    2   stalks celery, sliced
   5-6   green onions (white and green parts), sliced
    1   small green pepper, cut into 1-inch pieces
    1   small red pepper, cut into 1-inch pieces
   ¼   cup unsalted roasted peanuts, chopped
   ¼   cup fresh parsley or watercress, coarsely chopped
    1   bunch (about 1 ½ pounds) fresh broccoli, cut into stalks
    1   tablespoon sesame seeds
   ✿   *garnish:* pimento strips

Combine the rice and broth in a large saucepan; bring to a boil. Reduce the heat, cover, and simmer for 15 minutes until all the liquid has evaporated.

Heat olive oil in a skillet; sauté celery, onions, and peppers until tender. Add peanuts and parsley; combine with cooked rice. Keep warm or cover and chill until ready to serve.

Microwave broccoli in a microwave-safe bowl on HIGH for 6 to 7 minutes until tender.

Place sesame seeds on a baking sheet; toast in a 350 degree oven for 5 to 6 minutes, shaking the pan frequently to avoid burning the seeds. Remove the seeds from the pan; when cool, sprinkle over the broccoli.

Top rice and vegetable mixture with broccoli. Place in 350 degree oven until heated through. Garnish with pimento strips.

Serves 6
Per serving: 249 calories, 10 grams protein, 33 grams carbohydrate, 10 grams fat (34%), less than 1 milligram cholesterol, 310 milligrams sodium.

Good news: but if you ask me what it is, I know not;
It is a track of feet in the snow,
It is a lantern showing a path,
It is a door set open.
—G. K. CHESTERTON

CINNAMON-APPLE BREAD WITH YOGURT-CHEESE SPREAD

Holiday memories come from many things. For me, the fragrance of sweet spices warms the house along with hearth and hugs. Serve this apple ring as part of an irresistible holiday breakfast or brunch. Top it with the tasty spread for a lasting impression.

Filling:
1 ½ cups unsweetened applesauce
3 tablespoons brown sugar
¾ teaspoon apple-pie spice
1 tablespoon plus 1 teaspoon cornstarch
1 tablespoon vanilla extract

Dough:
1 package dry yeast
⅓ cup warm water (105 degrees to 115 degrees)
¾ teaspoon apple-pie spice
3 tablespoons sugar
¾ teaspoon salt
1 egg, beaten
½ cup skim milk, scalded
3 ¼ cups all-purpose flour, divided

Glaze:
¼ cup powdered sugar, sifted
1 teaspoon vanilla extract
1 ½ teaspoons water

Yogurt-Cheese Spread:
1 quart plain low-fat yogurt
½ cup crushed pineapple, drained well

For the filling: In a small saucepan, combine applesauce, brown sugar, and apple-pie spice; cook over medium heat for 20 minutes; stir frequently. Combine cornstarch and vanilla; add to the mixture. Stir until thickened (about 1 minute). Remove from heat and allow to cool.

For the dough: In a large bowl, dissolve yeast in warm water; let stand 5 minutes.

Add apple-pie spice, sugar, salt, and egg; stir well. Add milk; stir well. Gradually stir in 3 cups flour to make a stiff dough. Turn out onto a lightly floured surface. Knead dough until smooth and elastic (about 10 minutes). Add enough remaining flour to keep dough from sticking to surface.

Place dough in a large bowl coated with vegetable cooking spray, turning to coat entire surface. Cover and let rise in a warm place (85 degrees) until double (about 45 minutes).

Work dough down with a spoon. Turn out dough onto a lightly floured surface and roll into an 18-by-24-inch rectangle. Spread applesauce mixture over entire surface, leaving a ½-inch margin on one long side. Beginning at wide end, roll up jellyroll style; pinch seam to seal. (Do not seal ends.) Shape roll into circle by bringing ends together and sealing closed. With a knife, make 1-inch cuts about 3 inches apart, being careful not to cut clear through.

Cover and let rise in a warm place (85 degrees) until double (about 45 minutes). Bake at 375 degrees for 20 minutes. Remove from baking sheet; place on a wire rack.

For the glaze: Combine powdered sugar, vanilla, and water; drizzle over warm rolls.

For the Yogurt-Cheese Spread: Line colander with cheesecloth. Place yogurt in colander. Cover. Place colander over bowl to catch drippings. Refrigerate and drain for 8 to 10 hours. Remove from cheesecloth. Store in a covered container for up to 3 weeks. When ready to serve, combine 1 cup yogurt cheese and crushed pineapple; spread on bread.

Makes 2 dozen pieces when cut
Per serving: 101 calories, 3 grams protein, 21 grams carbohydrate, less than 1 gram fat (6%), 12 milligrams cholesterol, 36 milligrams sodium.

And sleepless children's hearts are glad, And Christmas morning bells say "Come!"
—SIR JOHN BETJEMAN

ELEGANT STUFFED POTATOES

MINTY CHOCOLATE MOUSSE

This is an elegant way to serve a baked potato. The flavor is full-bodied, but the fat content is not! You can prepare most of this dish ahead to save a little time.

    3 medium russet potatoes, scrubbed and
       baked
    ½ cup reduced-calorie cream cheese
    3 green onions (white and green parts),
       sliced
    ⅓ cup low-fat milk
    2 egg whites
    1 tablespoon Parmesan cheese, grated
    2 tablespoons fine dry bread crumbs
    2 teaspoons reduced-calorie margarine,
       melted
    ❧ *garnish:* additional green onion, sliced

Cut baked potatoes in half lengthwise and scoop out pulp, leaving a ¼-inch shell. Set shells aside.

Mash pulp with an electric mixer on low speed. Add cream cheese and onions. Add ¼ teaspoon salt and pepper, if desired, or to taste. While continuing to beat, gradually add enough of the milk to make potato mixture light and fluffy. Beat in egg whites. Spoon potato mixture into reserved potato shells.

Combine Parmesan cheese, dry bread crumbs, and margarine; sprinkle over potatoes. Place potatoes on an ungreased baking sheet. Bake in a 325 degree oven, uncovered, 10 minutes or until heated through. Garnish with sliced green onions.

Serves 6

Per serving: 147 calories, 5 grams protein, 20 grams carbohydrate, 5 grams fat (31%), 12 milligrams cholesterol, 136 milligrams sodium.

Nothing is more refreshing than the flavor of mint, especially when combined with the magnificent obsession—chocolate. Indulge without guilt when you eat this low-fat favorite.

    ½ cup sugar
    ½ cup unsweetened cocoa
    ¾ cup low-fat milk
    ¼ teaspoon mint extract
    2 teaspoons vanilla extract
    2 egg yolks
    3 egg whites, at room temperature
    1 cup nondairy whipped topping

Combine sugar and cocoa in a saucepan; stir well. Add milk; stir well. Place over medium heat; bring to a boil, stirring mixture constantly with a wire whisk. Spoon into a large bowl and add extracts; stir well. Cool completely.

Add egg yolks, one at a time, to cooled cocoa mixture; mix well. Set aside.

Beat egg whites at high speed of an electric mixer until stiff peaks form. Gently fold the egg whites into the whipped topping.

Stir about ⅓ of the cream mixture into the chocolate mixture, mixing thoroughly. Then scrape the remaining cream mixture over the chocolate base; gently fold them together. Pour the mousse into individual dessert cups or a serving bowl and refrigerate until set (about 2 hours).

Serves 4

Per 5 ounce serving: 254 calories, 9 grams protein, 37 grams carbohydrate, 10 grams fat (33%), 138 milligrams cholesterol, 102 milligrams sodium.

HEALTHFUL GIFTS OF GOOD TASTE

During the holidays, I often am inundated with gifts of candy, cookies, and other rich goodies. Granted, I appreciate the expression of love, and I eat my fair share. However, I try to avoid the sugar overload that accompanies the season. For a change of pace, why not give more healthful food gifts this year? They still can be homemade and reflect your thoughtfulness.

All of these gift ideas include one or two of the recipes found in this book. Just refer to the Index for page numbers.

- ❖ Fill a glass jar with ingredients for *Seven-Grain Cereal.* Layer the different varieties of grains for visual appeal. Be sure to include the directions for preparation.
- ❖ A loaf of *Easy Whole-Wheat Bread With Sunflower Seeds* or *Dill Bread* wrapped in colorful cellophane paper tied with contrasting ribbons makes a lasting impression.
- ❖ For the outdoor enthusiast, fill a backpack with camping necessities and a big bag full of *Granola.*
- ❖ Jars of *Fresh Basil-Tomato Sauce* tied with red ribbons look appetizing in a colander full of packaged pasta, dried Italian herbs, and a container of grated Parmesan cheese.
- ❖ Friends will appreciate a large container of *Store-and-Bake Bran Muffin* mix for a timesaving, delicious breakfast during the busy holidays.
- ❖ *Three-Apple Topping* makes a wonderful gift because it lasts for about 3 weeks in the refrigerator. Fill a jar and pack it along with a loaf of *Banana-Carrot Bread* or a batch of *Honey-Peach Bran Muffins.*
- ❖ Prepare a basket with the recipe and ingredients necessary for *Orange Cider*: apple juice, cloves, cinnamon sticks, and orange and spice herbal tea bags. Tie additional cinnamon sticks and lemon leaves with ribbon for a sweet smell.
- ❖ The holiday season is a perfect time for gathering beautiful citrus. Fill a large basket with a wide array of citrus varieties available: oranges, grapefruits, tangerines, kumquats, tangelos, pomelos. Include a recipe for *Citrus Medley With Apricot-Lemon Sauce.*
- ❖ Mix together the dry ingredients for *Minty Cocoa.* Package in an airtight container. The gift recipient only has to add milk and heat through. Attach peppermint candies to your gift for color and sparkle.
- ❖ Homemade *Basil Pesto Dip* is a great gift because it is so versatile. Give it by itself or mix it with the ricotta cheese as suggested in the recipe. Send along a tray of crunchy crackers and fresh cut vegetables.
- ❖ A bag of *Bagel Crisps,* a pound of your favorite cheese, fresh apples, and a bottle of sparkling cider creates an instant New Year's gift basket. Include cheese and apple slicers, plus all the party necessities: noisemakers, streamers, hats, and plastic toasting glasses.
- ❖ Jars of fresh *Gazpacho Dip* make a welcome gift for those fond of Mexican cuisine. Add a bag of *Crispy Tortilla Chips* with an invitation to dinner at your favorite Mexican restaurant.
- ❖ *Spiced Fruit Compote* looks beautiful packed in unusual-shaped jars or containers. Wrap with gold-trimmed ribbon and attach a sparkling tree ornament. Send along a batch of *Whole-Wheat Scones* to eat with the fruit.

A Matter of Fat

Fat supplies more than twice the amount of calories as protein or carbohydrate (1 gram = 9 calories). Despite the high calories, Americans are eating more fats now than ever before. In addition, the increased consumption of all kinds of fats is believed to contribute to heart disease. Along with a low-fiber diet, a high-fat diet is related to the incidence of certain forms of cancer. Just a few changes in your current dietary habits could greatly reduce your risk of these diseases. Here are the different kinds of fat.

CHOLESTEROL: Our body manufactures most of the cholesterol found in our blood. This cholesterol level is largely a matter of genetics. The rest comes from our diet. Animal products are the only source of this waxy substance, despite what some food labels say. A high-cholesterol, high-fat diet has been correlated with a high blood cholesterol that, in turn, increases the risk for heart disease.

SATURATED FAT: This blood cholesterol–raising fat is solid or semisolid at room temperature. It occurs primarily in animal products: egg yolks, meats, milk, and cheese. Certain vegetable fats called tropical oils also are saturated: coconut, palm, and palm kernel oils.

MONOUNSATURATED FAT: Recent studies indicate that monounsaturated fat may have a cholesterol-lowering effect. Find it in avocados, peanuts and peanut oil, olives and olive oil, canola oil, and most nuts—except walnuts, which are high in polyunsaturated fat. (See list below.)

POLYUNSATURATED FAT: This fat is often touted as the "good" fat because researchers report that it can lower blood cholesterol. But you cannot eat as much of it as you want. Like other fats, this fat should be used sparingly. When possible, substitute polyunsaturated fat, found most abundantly in plants, for saturated fat. Liquid at room temperature and even when refrigerated, this fat is an excellent source of linoleic acid, a nutrient needed for healthy skin and for blood pressure regulation. Find polyunsaturated fat in safflower, sunflower, corn, sesame, soy, and cottonseed oils.

Fats and oils are combinations of various types of fat, including saturated, monounsaturated, and polyunsaturated. A fat or oil is identified by the type of fat in greatest concentration. For example, canola oil contains 62 percent monounsaturated fat and is classified as a monounsaturate, even though other fats are present.

The following list ranks each fat, oil, or nut from the least to the greatest amount of saturated fat. Choose those fats near the top of the list more frequently.

Comparison of Dietary Fats*

Fat	Saturated (%)	Mono (%)	Poly (%)
Canola oil	6	62	32
Hazelnuts	7	81	11
Almonds	8	72	20
Safflower oil	10	13	77
Sunflower oil	11	20	69
Walnuts, English	11	16	71
Corn oil	13	25	61
Olive oil	14	77	9
Soybean oil	15	24	54
Peanuts	15	50	30

Comparison of Dietary Fats (continued)*

Fat	Saturated (%)	Mono (%)	Poly (%)
Peanut oil	18	49	33
Chestnuts	18	39	42
Margarine	19	49	32
Brazil nuts	27	34	39
Cottonseed	27	19	54
Vegetable shortening	28	44	28
Butter fat	66	30	4
Coconut	83	7	2

Composition of Foods, Agriculture Handbook No. 8-4 (Washington, D.C.: United States Department of Agriculture, 1979). *Comparison of Dietary Fats* (Proctor & Gamble, 1988).

MENU MAKEOVER

The surgeon general's Report on Nutrition and Health called overconsumption of fat a major health concern. Conforming to the dictate while pleasing the palate is a difficult challenge.

Many recipes can be modified without significantly altering quality. Ask yourself the following questions before altering any recipe:

1. What kind of fat and how much is being used? Try substituting polyunsaturated or mono-unsaturated fat for the cholesterol-raising saturated fat. You can use reduced-calorie margarine when butter, lard, shortening, or margarine is called for. Use just a little bit more of the lower calorie version because it is higher in water content. Instead of heavy creams, use light cream, evaporated low-fat milk, or low-fat milk. A combination of any of these is a moderate approach. Combine yogurt with half the mayonnaise or whipped topping when preparing dressings or toppings. Blended cottage and ricotta cheese combinations also lower fat totals.

2. What does the fat do? In some cases, the fat is used to enhance flavor, as with sautéing. It can be used to thicken texture or to bind ingredients, as in adding egg yolks or heavy cream. Use moderation; don't feel that you have to eliminate all fat, but if the rest of the meal is relatively high in fat, then consider using an alternative. Reducing amounts rather than eliminating the ingredient altogether maintains flavor, as with cheeses, nuts, and seeds.

3. Can another method of preparation be used? If directions call for sautéing vegetables, would braising or microwaving work just as well? Or perhaps you could sauté in a low-fat liquid such as soy sauce, vegetable broth, or water.

Feasting on Fiber

Getting enough fiber in your diet is important, but too much of a good thing can be hazardous to your health. An adequate amount of fiber (20 to 35 grams per day) may help reduce your risk of colon cancer. More than this may interfere with mineral absorption.

If you would like to increase your fiber intake, start adding gradually. A sudden increase in high-fiber foods can cause intestinal upset and blockage. Begin with 10 grams per day for a week; then increase to 15 grams per day for another week, until you reach the recommended amount.

Fiber comes in two types: soluble and insoluble. You'll find insoluble fiber in wheat and corn brans and vegetables. Soluble fiber is present in oats, barley, rice, fruits, and legumes.

Refer to the following list to help you get the recommended amount. Be sure to include both types of fiber in your diet.

Crackers and Cereals

	Fiber (grams)		Fiber (grams)
RyKrisp (2 triple)	3	Bran flake type (1-ounce serving)	4 to 8
Cracker bread (2)	2	Oatmeal (1-ounce serving)	2
All-Bran type (1-ounce serving)	10 to 12		

Glorious Greens and Beans

	Fiber (grams)		Fiber (grams)
Baked beans with tomato sauce (½ cup cooked)	9	Lentils, peas (½ cup cooked)	4
Kidney beans (½ cup cooked)	7	Corn (½ cup cooked)	3
Lima beans, pinto beans, and split peas (½ cup cooked)	5	Potato with skin, sweet potato (1 medium)	3
		Broccoli, Brussels sprouts, carrots, spinach, zucchini (½ cup cooked)	2

Fiber-Filled Fruits

	Fiber (grams)		Fiber (grams)
Blackberries (½ cup)	5	Raspberries (½ cup)	3
Pear with skin (1 medium)	5	Strawberries (1 cup)	3
Apple with skin (1 medium)	4	Apricots (3 medium)	2
Prunes (4)	4	Banana (1 medium)	2
Honeydew (¼ medium)	3	Blueberries (½ cup)	2
Orange (1 medium)	3	Dates (3)	2
Raisins (¼ cup)	3	Peach with skin (1 medium)	2

Best Breads and Pasta

	Fiber (grams)		Fiber (grams)
Whole-wheat spaghetti (1 cup cooked)	4	Whole-wheat pancakes (2)	3
Bran muffin (1 medium)	3	Whole-wheat blueberry muffin (1 medium)	2
Buckwheat pancakes (2)	3	Brown rice (1 cup cooked)	2
Whole-wheat bread (2 slices)	3		

GRAZING ON GRAINS

Barley: Whole polished kernels with bland flavor and soft texture. Barley, like oats and legumes, is a good source of water-soluble fiber. Use in soups, with vegetables or fruits. Cook 1 part barley to 2 parts water for 45 minutes.

Buckwheat or kasha: Whole kernels with mild nutty flavor and soft texture. Kasha is roasted buckwheat and the flavor is nuttier. Use buckwheat in Russian dishes or pilafs. Cook 1 part buckwheat to 2 parts water for 15 minutes.

Cornmeal: Ground corn kernels, white or yellow. Cornmeal is sweet and soft. Use in cereals, polenta, and in baking. Cook 1 part cornmeal to 4 parts water for 30 minutes.

Couscous: Flour-coated semolina, which is ground durum wheat. Almost all couscous in the United States is instant. Serve couscous like rice. Cooking procedures vary with brand.

Hominy: Skinned white corn kernels that are slightly sweet and firm. Use in cereals or side dishes. Cook 1 part hominy to 3 parts water for 2 to 3 hours.

Hominy grits (ground hominy): Available in coarse, medium, and fine textures. Use in cereals and baking. Cook 1 part hominy to 4 parts water for 30 minutes.

Millet: Small, tan whole kernels. Millet has a delicate, sweet, nutty flavor and is rich in minerals. Serve millet like rice; use in soups. Cook 1 part millet to 2 parts water for 35 minutes.

Oat groats: Whole-oat grain with nutty flavor and chewy texture. Oat groats are predominantly used in cereals. Cook 1 part groats to 2 parts water for 1 hour.

Oatmeal: Steamed, flattened, and flakes or cut oat groats. Oatmeal has a slightly nutty flavor and soft texture. It is a highly water-soluble fiber. Use for cereal and baking. Cook 1 part oatmeal to 2 parts water. Times vary for rolled or quick-cooking.

Oats, steel-cut (Scottish or Irish): Sliced oat groats with a nutty flavor and firm texture. Best used for cereal and baking. Cook 1 part oats to 2 parts water for 30 minutes.

Quinoa (pronounced keen wa): Pale yellow seed slightly larger than a mustard seed. Quinoa has a sweet flavor and soft texture, and is rich in calcium. Serve it like rice or as a base for salads. Cook 1 part quinoa to 2 parts water for 12 minutes.

Rice, instant (white or brown): Precooked, dehydrated long-grain white or brown rice. White variety has a relatively bland taste and soft texture; brown rice has a nutty flavor and soft texture. Instant rice is best used in side dishes, salads, pilafs, and casseroles. Cooking procedures will vary among brands.

Rice, Italian short-grain (arborio): Polished white kernels that are rectangular in shape. It has a bland taste and soft texture. This rice is predominantly used in risotto. Cook 1 part rice to 2 parts water for 20 minutes.

Rice, medium- and long-grain (white or brown): White is polished kernels; brown has the bran intact and is more nutritious. White has a bland flavor and firm texture, while the brown has a nutty flavor and firm texture. Use in side dishes, salads, pilafs, and casseroles. Cook 1 part white rice to 2 parts water for 15 minutes; 30 to 40 minutes for brown.

Rice, wild: Not really a rice at all, but a seed of a native grass. Wild rice has an intense, nutty flavor and firm, chewy texture. Best used in salads, side dishes, pilafs, and stuffing. Cook 1 part wild rice to 3 parts water for 45 minutes.

Rye: Whole rye kernels with sour taste and soft texture. Rye is high in potassium and riboflavin. Use in cereals, stews, and breads. Cook 1 part grain to 3 parts water for 45 minutes.

Wheat berries: Unprocessed whole-wheat kernels; hearty flavor and chewy texture. Use in salads and baking. Cook 1 part wheat berries to 2 parts water for 1 hour.

Wheat bran: Outer coating of wheat seed or germ, high in insoluble fiber. Use in baking, as a topping or as a thickening agent. No cooking time.

Wheat, bulgur: Cracked wheat, hulled, steamed, and dried. It has a nutty flavor and soft texture. Serve like rice. Cook 1 part bulgur to 2 parts water for 40 minutes.

Wheat, cracked: Crushed whole-wheat kernels with hearty flavor and firm texture. Use primarily in cereals and breads. Cook 1 part grain to 2 parts water for 40 minutes.

Wheat germ: Seed of wheat kernel that is high in vitamin B's (thiamin, riboflavin, and niacin). Use wheat germ in baking, as a topping or as a thickening agent. Purchase toasted.

GLOSSARY OF GREENS

Arugula: Small, tender, and pungent. This green resembles radish tops. The elongated, smooth, dark green leaves grow in clusters. The peppery taste is best combined with sweet or bitter greens.

Belgian endive: Spear-shaped leaves that are pale green with slightly ruffled yellow edges. The texture is crisp and juicy; the flavor is slightly bitter. Handles sweet, full-bodied dressings.

Bibb: A small version of Boston lettuce whose loosely furled green leaves are darker and have a crunchier texture. Its delicate, sweet flavor complements mild dressings.

Boston butter: Moderately sized with loosely furled, pale green leaves. Use a light dressing on this mild green.

Cabbage: Green, red, and Chinese varieties. Green and red have tough, crisp, strongly flavored leaves; Chinese has crinkly leaves on a thick stem with a more delicate flavor. High in vitamin C. Best served with creamy citrus or poppy seed dressings.

Chicory (curly endive): Lacy, dark green outer leaves with tender inner ones. Use these in salads with bitter greens and a robust vinaigrette.

Escarole: A type of chicory. This large head has dark green leaves with a pale yellow heart. Its bitter flavor is best paired with sweet vinaigrettes in mixed green salads.

Iceberg: Most common lettuce. The crisp, cool leaves have a crunchy texture and mild flavor. Serve with full-flavored dressings.

Leaf or red leaf: Frilly-edged leaves, delicate in texture and mild and sweet in flavor. Serve in mixed green salads with lightly textured dressings.

Mâche or lamb's lettuce: Light or deep green leaves that grow in a delicate cluster. Its flavor is sweet and nutty. It is expensive and very perishable. A light vinaigrette is best.

Oakleaf: Large, loosely arranged red or green leaves resembling oak leaves. They have a sweet flavor. Serve with light dressings.

Radicchio: A type of chicory resembling red cabbage. Its tightly packed purplish-red leaves are bittersweet in flavor. Combine with other greens for a splash of color. Use with robust dressings.

Romaine: Crisp, oblong, dark green leaves surrounding tender, pale yellow leaves. The outer leaves have a sweet, nutty flavor. Stands up well to bold combinations, as in Caesar Salad. Adds interest to mixed green salads.

Spinach: Tender, dark green leaves, curly or flat, with a mild flavor. Supplies abundant iron, potassium, vitamins A and C, and calcium. Use raw in salads or in stir-fried and other cooked dishes.

Watercress: Tender, dark green leaves with a peppery flavor. Rich in vitamins A and C. Combine with other bitter greens and mild dressings or use in soups or as garnishes.

LIVING ON LEGUMES

Beans, lentils, and peas are part of a larger food group known as legumes. The wonderful thing about legumes is that they contain as much protein as beef, chicken, and fish. Just 4 percent of their calories comes from fat. The rest of the calories in legumes come from complex carbohydrates, which are energy producing. Don't forget about legumes' healthful amounts of vitamins A and B_6, iron, potassium, calcium, and phosphorus.

Meatless menus rely heavily on legumes for protein; however, the protein in legumes is incomplete. They do not contain all 9 essential amino acids necessary for protein function and must combine with a protein complement. This can be grains, seeds, nuts, and some vegetables, or a complete protein provided by dairy products (see Complementary Protein, p. 150). All of the menus in this book provide complete protein due to combinations of incomplete proteins.

The following guide contains brief descriptions of the most popular legume varieties, along with ways to best serve them.*

Black, Cuban, or turtle beans: These medium-size black-skinned ovals have a rich, sweet taste. They are best served in Mexican and Latin American dishes or thick soups and stews.

Black-eyed peas: These are small and oval-shaped, creamy white with a black spot. They have a vegetable flavor with mealy texture. Use in salads with rice and greens.

Garbanzo beans or chickpeas: These legumes are large, round, and tan-colored. They have a nutty flavor and crunchy texture. Use in soups, stews, and puréed for dips.

Great northern beans: This variety is medium-white and kidney-shaped. Enjoy the delicate flavor and firm texture in salads, soups, and main dishes.

Kidney beans: These familiar beans are large, red, and kidney-shaped; the white variety is called cannellini. They have a bland taste and soft texture, but tough skins. Use in chili, bean stews, and Mexican dishes for red; Italian dishes for white.

Lentils: These legumes are small, flat, and round. Usually brown-colored, lentils also can be green, pink, or red. They have a mild taste with firm texture. Best used when combined with grains or vegetables in salads, soups, or stews.

Lima or butter beans: Limas are soft and mealy in texture. They are flat, oval-shaped, and white tinged with green. The smaller variety has a milder taste. Use in soups and/or stews.

Pinto beans: These medium ovals are mottled beige and brown with an earthy flavor. They are most often used in Mexican dishes, such as refried beans, stews, or dips.

Red beans: This versatile bean is a medium-size, dark red oval. The taste and texture are similar to kidney beans. Use in soups and stews, with rice.

Soybeans: You can find these creamy white ovals in numerous food products, such as tofu, flour, grits, or milk. They have a firm texture and bland flavor. The fat content of soybeans is the highest of all legumes.

Split peas: Green or yellow, these small halved peas supply an earthy flavor with mealy texture. They are best used in soups and with rice or grains.

White, small white, navy beans: These beans are small white ovals and are best used in soups, stews, and baked beans.

* All the legumes in this guide, except lentils and split peas, require at least 8 hours of soaking overnight. After soaking, rinse and cover with fresh water. Then, bring to a boil; simmer for 1 to 2 hours or until soft. Lentils and split peas require about 30 to 50 minutes to soften.

PROTEIN PUNCH

A big concern for non-vegetarians is whether a vegetarian diet will provide enough protein. The answer is a resounding yes! Most people do not realize that in the United States, we eat almost twice as much protein as the Recommended Daily Allowance (RDA) suggests. For men, the RDA is 56 grams. Non-vegetarian men eat an average of 103 grams per day. Vegetarian men, surprisingly, eat an average of 105 grams per day.

The RDA for women is around 44 grams. Non-vegetarian women consume an average of 74 grams per day while vegetarian women eat an average of 63 grams per day.

From a nutritional point of view, one could argue that these numbers don't necessarily reflect the quality of protein consumed. Animal protein contains the complete set of essential amino acids, the building blocks of protein. These amino acids are needed for a multitude of biological functions. Vegetable protein, on the other hand, contains only portions of the set. But the American Dietetic Association made it very clear in its 1987 and revised 1992 position paper on the adequacy of vegetarian diets that "plant sources of protein alone can provide adequate amounts of the essential and nonessential amino acids, assuming that dietary protein sources from plants are reasonably varied and that caloric intake is sufficient to meet energy needs." The position goes on to state that conscious combining of foods within a meal is unnecessary.

If anything, Americans need to cut down on the amount of protein consumed. Although most vegetarian diets meet or exceed the RDA for protein, they often provide less protein than non-vegetarian diets. Colin Campbell, a researcher from Cornell University, has suggested that a lower protein intake may be associated with better calcium absorption and retention in vegetarians. Also, a lower protein diet may result in a lower fat intake because foods high in protein are often high in fat. A low-fat diet has been shown to increase the incidence of coronary heart disease and some types of cancer.

Consider the following guidelines when planning a protein-adequate diet:
- ❖ Include a variety of legumes, daily products, whole grains and dark leafy greens.
- ❖ Pair beans and legumes with vegetables or fruits high in vitamin C to enhance the absorption of iron. Iron is also found in dried cereals and leafy greens.
- ❖ Add soy protein to recipes more often. It has been shown to be nutritionally equal in protein value to proteins of animal origin.
- ❖ Choose low-fat dairy products as a source of protein. Low-fat dairy foods contain as much calcium, Vitamin D and protein as their high-fat counterparts.

Grocery Guide

Fruits (fresh)

Apples	6 small (1 ½ pounds)	4 cups sliced or 4 ½ cups chopped
Apricots	6 to 8 medium (1 pound)	2 cups chopped
Bananas	4 small (1 pound)	2 cups mashed
Cantaloupe	1 average (2 pounds)	3 cups cubed
Cherries	2 cups	1 cup pitted
Cranberries	1 pound	4 ½ cups raw
Figs	4 small (1 pound)	2 cups chopped
Grapefruit	1 small (1 pound)	1 cup sectioned
Grapes, Thompson seedless	40 grapes (¼ pound)	2 cups halved
Lemons	2 medium (½ pound)	6 tablespoons juice or 1 tablespoon grated zest
Limes	5 medium (½ pound)	4 tablespoons juice or 1 tablespoon grated zest
Oranges	3 medium (1 pound)	3 cups sectioned
Papaya	1 pound	2 cups cubed or 1 cup puréed
Peaches	3 medium (1 pound)	2 cups chopped
Pears	3 medium (1 pound)	2 cups chopped
Pineapple	1 medium (3 pounds)	2 ½ cups chopped
Strawberries	4 cups whole	4 cups sliced
Tangerines	4 medium (1 pound)	2 cups sectioned

Fruits (dried)

Apples	1 pound	8 cups diced
Apricots	1 pound	8 cups diced
Figs	2 ½ cups (1 pound)	4 ½ cups whole cooked or 2 cups chopped raw
Pears	3 cups (1 pound)	5 ½ cups cooked
Prunes, pitted	2 ½ cups (1 pound)	3 ¾ cups cooked
Raisins, seedless	2 ¾ cups (1 pound)	3 ¾ cups cooked or 2 cups chopped raw

Vegetables

Beans, green	1 pound	5 cups 1-inch pieces raw
Beets	1 pound	6 cups sliced raw or 2 ½ cups sliced cooked
Bell pepper	3 medium (1 pound)	2 cups chopped raw or 4 cups sliced raw
Broccoli	2 stalks (1 pound)	6 cups chopped cooked
Cabbage	1 medium head (2 ½ pounds)	10 cups shredded raw or 3 cups sliced raw
Carrots	6 medium (1 pound)	3 cups sliced cooked
Cauliflower	1 medium head (1 ½ pounds)	6 cups chopped cooked
Celery	½ pound	1 ½ cups chopped raw
	1 stalk	½ cup chopped raw
Corn	6 ears	2 ½ cups cut raw
Cucumber	1 medium (½ pound)	1 ½ cups sliced raw or 1 cup diced raw
Eggplant	1 medium (1 pound)	12 (¼-inch) slices raw or 6 cups cubed raw
Garlic	1 clove	1 teaspoon chopped raw
Leeks, white part only	½ pound	2 cups chopped raw or 1 cup chopped cooked
Lettuce	1 medium head (1 ½ pounds)	6 cups bite-size pieces
Mushrooms	½ pound	2 cups sliced raw
Onion	1 medium (½ pound)	1 cup chopped raw or 1 ½ cups sliced raw
Onion, green	6 medium (¼ pound)	1 cup chopped raw
Parsley	2 ounces	1 cup tightly packed raw or 1 cup chopped raw
Pimento	1 (4-ounce) jar	½ cup chopped
Potatoes	2 medium russet or 6 to 8 new (1 pound)	2 ½ cups diced cooked or 3 cups chopped or sliced
Pumpkin	1 medium (3 pounds)	4 cups cooked and mashed
Spinach	1 pound	4 cups bite-size pieces or 1 ½ cups cooked

Squash,		
Acorn	1 medium (1 ½ pounds)	2 cups cooked mashed
Banana	1 medium (3 pounds)	4 cups cooked mashed
Spaghetti	1 medium (5 pounds)	8 cups cooked
Summer	4 medium (1 pound)	1 cup chopped cooked
Zucchini	2 medium (1 pound)	1 cup chopped cooked or 2 cups diced raw
Tomatilloes	4 small or 2 large (¼ pound)	1 cup chopped raw
Tomatoes	3 medium (1 pound)	2 cups chopped raw or 1 ¼ cups chopped cooked
Watercress	1 bunch (¼ pound)	1 cup loosely packed raw

Legumes

Garbanzo beans	1 pound	2 cups dry, 6 cups cooked
Kidney beans	1 pound	1 ½ cups dry, 4 cups cooked
Lentils	½ pound	1 cup dry, 2 cups cooked
Lima or navy beans	1 pound	2 ½ cups dry, 6 cups cooked

Pasta

Chinese noodles	¾ pound	5 cups cooked
Linguine	1 pound	5 cups cooked
Macaroni	1 pound	3 cups dry, 12 cups cooked
Spaghetti	1 pound	8 cups cooked

Nuts

Almonds	4 ounces shelled	1 cup whole or 1 ½ cups chopped
Peanuts	1 pound in shell	1 ¼ cups whole or 1 cup chopped
Pecans	4 ounces shelled	1 cup whole or 1 ½ cups chopped
Walnuts	1 pound in shell	2 cups whole or 2 ½ cups chopped

Spices and Herbs

Apple-pie spice	1 tablespoon	2 teaspoons cinnamon and 1 teaspoon nutmeg and dash of allspice
Garlic	2 cloves	2 teaspoons minced raw or ¼ teaspoon powder
Herbs	1 tablespoon fresh	1 teaspoon dried
Italian herb blend	1 tablespoon	1 ½ teaspoons dried oregano and ¾ teaspoon each dried basil and thyme
Pumpkin-pie spice	1 tablespoon	2 teaspoons ground cinnamon and 1 teaspoon each ground nutmeg and ginger and dash cloves

Dairy Products and Eggs

Buttermilk	1 cup	1 tablespoon lemon juice and low-fat milk to make 1 cup
Cheese	¼ pound	1 cup grated
Cottage cheese	½ pound	1 cup
Egg whites	8 medium	1 cup raw
Eggs	6 medium	1 cup whole raw
	1 medium	2 egg whites
Instant nonfat powdered milk	⅓ cup plus ⅔ cup water	1 cup liquid milk

INDEX OF RECIPES

Appetizers and Dips
Basil Pesto Dip With
    Crackers, 120
Creamy Cherry Dip, 39
Creamy Spinach Dip, 29
Gazpacho Dip, 76
Italian Stuffed Artichokes, 49
Pinwheels and Pencils, 40

Beverages
Apricot Cider, 63
Apricot Refresher, 134
Caribbean Quencher, 75
Citrus-Banana Wake-up, 45
Cranberry-Apple Soda, 91
50-50 Shake, 84
Grape Cider, 88
Kay's Almond Drink, 102
Orange Cider, 127
Orange-Peach Frost, 136
Minty Cocoa, 119
Pineapple-Banana Slush, 121
Tomato Cocktail, 110

Breads and Muffins
Almond-Pumpkin Muffins
    With Streusel Topping, 107
Bagel Crisps, 34
Banana-Carrot Bread, 73
Bran Muffins With
    Blueberries, 44
Cinnamon-Apple Bread With
    Yogurt-Cheese Spread, 139
Date-Filled Ring, 128
Dill Bread, 116
Easy Whole-Wheat Bread With
    Sunflower Seeds, 93
French Bread Round, 61
Honey-Peach Bran Muffins, 18

Parmesan Breadstick
    Twists, 130
Rustic Corn Bread, 29
Store-and-Bake Bran
    Muffins, 124
Whole-Wheat Potato Bread, 57
Whole-Wheat Scones, 111

Cakes and Cookies
Banana Snack Cake, 134
Blueberry Cheesecake, 58
Chunky Apple and Peanut
    Butter Cookies, 82
Cookie Baskets, 68
Oatmeal Cookie Sandwiches
    and Raisin Sauce, 102
Sunny Carrot Cake With
    Yogurt-Cheese Frosting, 92
Texas Chocolate Sheet Cake
    With Fudge Frosting, 114

Desserts
Apple-Pear Crisp and Yogurt
    Dessert Sauce, 97
Apricot-Raisin Bars, 88
Baked Apple Cages, 40
Bananas Foster, 52
Chewy Mint-Fudge
    Brownies, 30
Couscous Pudding With
    Raspberry Sauce, 119
Flan, 77
Fresh Raspberry Yogurt in
    Cookie Baskets, 68
Layered Lemon Angel Dessert
    and Strawberry Sauce, 26
Minty Chocolate Mousse, 140
Sweetheart Strawberry
    Mousse, 18

Tropical Strawberry Sherbet, 35
Watermelon Sorbet, 72

Dressings
Creamy Dill Dressing, 71
Creamy Herb Dressing, 66
Feta Dressing, 61
Grapefruit Dressing, 133
Grapefruit Vinaigrette, 16
Herb Dressing, 37
Lime–Poppy Seed Dressing, 98
Orange-Raspberry
    Vinaigrette, 24
Sweet Savory Dressing, 82
Tofu-Honey Dressing, 86
Watercress Dressing, 116

Entrees
Enchiladas Monterey, 76
Garden-Topped Potatoes, 66
Greek Salad–Filled French
    Bread Round, 61
Green Pepper Cups Stuffed
    With Garden Vegetable
    Pilaf, 96
Vegetable and Tofu Stir-Fry, 50
Vegetable Stroganoff, 121

Entrees, Egg and/or Cheese
Artichoke-Spinach Bake, 100
Broccoli and Cheese Quiche, 16
Broccoli Calzone and Marinara
    Sauce, 85
Cheese and Egg Puff, 127
Egg Salad Sandwiches, 39
Enchiladas Monterey, 76
Omelet Primavera and Orange
    Sauce, 43
Pita Pizzas, 82

Spinach-Tofu Lasagna, 111
Summer Squash Soufflé, 56
Sweet Onion and Blended
    Cheese Pizza, 133
Tender Spinach Crepes and
    Fresh Basil-Tomato Sauce, 25
Tomato-Spinach-Mozzarella
    Sandwiches, 89

Salads

Apple-Nut Salad and Tofu-
    Honey Dressing, 86
Apricot-Cilantro Salad, 77
Berry-Banana Salad Mold, 103
Black and White Bean Salad
    With Feta Cheese, 69
Blushing Pink on Tender
    Greens and Grapefruit
    Vinaigrette, 16
Cabbage-Apple Salad and
    Sweet Savory Dressing, 82
Carrot, Raisin, and Orange
    Salad, 50
Citrus Medley With Apricot-
    Lemon Sauce, 128
Fresh Fruit and Blue Cheese
    Salad With Grapefruit
    Dressing, 133
Fresh Fruit Nestled in Barley
    Salad, 25
Fruit Salad and Creamy Yogurt
    Topping, 52
Good Earth Salad, 57
Greek Salad With Feta
    Dressing, 61
Holiday Cranberry Salad, 136
Italian Stuffed Artichokes, 49
Marinated Avocado Salad, 121
Marinated Corn Salad, 89
Medley of Baby Greens and
    Orange-Raspberry
    Vinaigrette, 24
Mixed Greens 'N Things
    Salad, 110

Spiced Fruit Compote, 103
Spinach Salad With Lime–
    Poppy Seed Dressing, 98
Sun Country Tomato Salad, 67
Sweet Onion–Potato Salad, 71
Three-Bean Salad With
    Artichoke Hearts, 86
Tofu–Snap Pea Salad and
    Creamy Herb Dressing, 66
Winter Greens Salad and
    Watercress Dressing, 116

Salads, Pasta

Enchanted Forest Pasta and
    Herb Dressing, 37
Garden Pasta Salad and
    Creamy Dill Dressing, 71
Spring-Green Tortellini
    Salad, 33
Tropical Fruit Pasta, 30

Sauces, Spreads, and Toppings

Apricot-Lemon Sauce, 128
Creamy Yogurt Topping, 52
Crunchy Apricot Topping, 34
Fresh Basil-Tomato Sauce, 25
Fudge Frosting, 114
Marinara Sauce, 85
Orange Sauce, 43
Raisin Sauce, 102
Raspberry Sauce, 119
Strawberry Sauce, 26
Streusel Topping, 107
Three-Apple Topping, 114
Yogurt-Cheese Frosting, 92
Yogurt-Cheese Spread, 139
Yogurt Dessert Sauce, 97

Side Dishes, Fruit, Grain, and Vegetable

Crispy Tortilla Chips, 115
Dried Fruit and Nut
    Dressing, 106

Elegant Stuffed Potatoes, 140
Festive Broccoli-Topped
    Holiday Rice, 137
Fresh Asparagus Bundles and
    Crunchy Apricot
    Topping, 34
Fresh Fruit Kabobs and Creamy
    Cherry Dip, 39
Garden Vegetable
    Casserole, 106
Granola, 63
Green Beans With Blue Cheese
    and Almonds, 56
Grilled Summer Vegetables, 72
Herbed Parmesan
    Tomatoes, 100
Honey-Lime Mango, 34
Mexican Vegetables and
    Gazpacho Dip, 76
Rice Acapulco, 75
Rice and Red Beans, 63
Seven-Grain Cereal and Fresh
    Fruit Medley, 44
Spiced Couscous in
    Cantaloupe, 67
Spiced Fruit Compote, 103
Sweet Potato Pancakes, 125
Two-Potato Twirls, 107
Unforgettable Baked Beans, 27

Soups

Autumn Vegetable Soup, 97
Berry-Peach Soup, 53
Chilled Green Bean Bisque, 65
Corn Chowder, 81
Cream of Potato and Watercress
    Soup, 130
Hearty Quick or Slow Stew, 115
Minestrone Soup, 60
Pumpkin and Potato Soup in
    Acorn Squash, 91
Spring Garden Vegetable
    Soup, 22
Sweet Pea Pod Soup, 15

INDEX OF INGREDIENTS

Apple
Apple-Nut Salad, 86
Apple-Pear Crisp, 97
Baked Apple Cages, 40
Cabbage-Apple Salad, 82
Carrot, Raisin, and Orange
    Salad, 50
Chunky Apple and Peanut-
    Butter Cookies, 82
Cinnamon-Apple Bread, 139
Cranberry-Apple Soda, 91
Fresh Fruit Kabobs, 39
Fresh Fruit Nestled in Barley
    Salad, 25
Three-Apple Topping, 114

Apricot
Apricot Cider, 63
Apricot-Cilantro Salad, 77
Apricot-Lemon Sauce, 128
Apricot-Raisin Bars, 88
Apricot Refresher, 134
Crunchy Apricot Topping, 34
Spiced Fruit Compote, 103

Artichoke
Artichoke-Spinach Bake, 100
Italian Stuffed Artichokes, 49
Spring-Green Tortellini
    Salad, 33
Three-Bean Salad With
    Artichoke Hearts, 86

Asparagus
Fresh Asparagus Bundles, 34
Omelet Primavera With Orange
    Sauce, 43
Spring Garden Vegetable
    Soup, 22

Avocado
Marinated Avocado Salad, 121

Bananas
Banana-Carrot Bread, 73
Bananas Foster, 52
Banana Snack Cake, 134
Berry-Banana Salad Mold, 103
Citrus-Banana Wake-up, 45
Fresh Fruit Kabobs, 39
Fresh Fruit Medley, 44
Pineapple-Banana Slush, 121
Tropical Fruit Pasta, 30
Tropical Strawberry Sherbet, 35

Barley
Fresh Fruit Nestled in Barley
    Salad, 25

Basil
Basil Pesto Dip, 120
Fresh Basil-Tomato Sauce, 25
Marinara Sauce, 85

Beans
Black and White Bean Salad
    With Feta Cheese, 69
Enchiladas Monterey, 76
Greek Salad, 61
Hearty Quick or Slow Stew, 115
Living on Legumes, 149
Rice and Red Beans, 63
Three-Bean Salad With
    Artichoke Hearts, 86
Unforgettable Baked Beans, 27

Blueberries
Blueberry Cheesecake, 58
Bran Muffins With
    Blueberries, 44

Bran
Bran Muffins With
    Blueberries, 44
Honey-Peach Bran Muffins, 18
Store-and-Bake Bran
    Muffins, 124

Broccoli
Broccoli and Cheese Quiche, 16
Broccoli Calzone and Marinara
    Sauce, 85
Enchanted Forest Pasta, 37
Festive Broccoli-Topped
    Holiday Rice, 137
Garden Pasta Salad, 71
Garden Vegetable
    Casserole, 106
Vegetable Stroganoff, 121

Bulgur
Good Earth Salad, 57

Cabbage
Cabbage-Apple Salad, 82
Vegetable and Tofu Stir-Fry, 50

Carrot
Banana-Carrot Bread, 73
Carrot, Raisin, and Orange
    Salad, 50
Enchanted Forest Pasta, 37
Garden Pasta Salad, 71
Garden Vegetable
    Casserole, 106
Mexican Vegetables, 76
Spring Garden Vegetable
    Soup, 22
Spring-Green Tortellini
    Salad, 33
Sunny Carrot Cake, 92
Vegetable Stroganoff, 121

Cauliflower
Garden Vegetable
Casserole, 106
Vegetable Stroganoff, 121

Cheese
Basil Pesto Dip, 120
Black and White Bean Salad
With Feta Cheese, 69
Blueberry Cheesecake, 58
Broccoli and Cheese Quiche, 16
Broccoli Calzone and Marinara
Sauce, 85
Cheese and Egg Puff, 127
Elegant Stuffed Potatoes, 140
Enchiladas Monterey, 76
Feta Dressing, 61
Fresh Fruit and Blue Cheese
Salad, 133
Garden Vegetable
Casserole, 106
Green Beans With Blue Cheese
and Almonds, 56
Green Pepper Cups Stuffed
With Garden Vegetable
Pilaf, 96
Herbed Parmesan
Tomatoes, 100
Italian Stuffed Artichokes, 49
Parmesan Breadstick
Twists, 130
Pita Pizzas, 82
Summer Squash Soufflé, 56
Sweet Onion and Blended
Cheese Pizza, 133
Tender Spinach Crepes, 25
Tomato-Spinach-Mozzarella
Sandwiches, 89

Cocoa
Chewy Mint Fudge
Brownies, 30
Fudge Frosting, 114
Minty Chocolate Mousse, 140

Minty Cocoa, 119
Texas Chocolate Sheet
Cake, 114

Corn
Corn Chowder, 81
Grilled Summer Vegetables, 72
Marinated Corn Salad, 89
Rustic Corn Bread, 29

Couscous
Couscous Pudding, 119
Spiced Couscous in
Cantaloupe, 67

Cranberry
Berry-Banana Salad Mold, 103
Cranberry-Apple Soda, 91
50-50 Shake, 84
Holiday Cranberry Salad, 136

Dates
Date-Filled Ring, 128

Dill
Creamy Dill Dressing, 71
Dill Bread, 116
Egg Salad Sandwiches, 39

Egg
Artichoke-Spinach Bake, 100
Broccoli and Cheese Quiche, 16
Cheese and Egg Puff, 127
Egg Salad Sandwiches, 39
Flan, 77
Omelet Primavera, 43
Summer Squash Soufflé, 56

Eggplant
Grilled Summer Vegetables, 72

Fat
A Matter of Fat, 144
Introduction, 10
Menu Makeover, 145

Fiber
Feasting on Fiber, 146
Introduction, 10

Grains (see specific grain)
Granola, 63
Grazing on Grains, 147
Seven-Grain Cereal, 44

Grape
Grape Cider, 88
Holiday Cranberry Salad, 136

Grapefruit
Blushing Pink on Tender
Greens, 16
Citrus Medley, 128
Fresh Fruit and Blue Cheese
Salad, 133
Grapefruit Dressing, 133
Grapefruit Vinaigrette, 16

Green Bean
Chilled Green Bean Bisque, 65
Green Beans With Blue Cheese
and Almonds, 56
Three-Bean Salad With
Artichoke Hearts, 86

Green or Red Pepper
Green Pepper Cups Stuffed
With Garden Vegetable
Pilaf, 96
Grilled Summer Vegetables, 72
Mexican Vegetables, 76

Greens
Apricot Cilantro Salad, 77
Blushing Pink on Tender
Greens, 16
Fresh Fruit and Blue Cheese
Salad, 133
Glossary of Greens, 148
Greek Salad, 61
Marinated Avocado Salad, 121

Medley of Baby Greens, 24
Mixed Greens 'N Things
    Salad, 110
Spinach Salad, 98
Winter Greens Salad, 116

Lemon
Apricot-Lemon Sauce, 128
Layered Lemon Angel Dessert
    and Strawberry Sauce, 26

Lentils
Good Earth Salad, 57
Hearty Quick or Slow Stew, 115
Living on Legumes, 150

Mango
Caribbean Quencher, 75
Honey-Lime Mango, 34

Melon
Fresh Fruit Nestled in Barley
    Salad, 25
Fruit Salad, 52
Spiced Couscous in
    Cantaloupe, 67
Watermelon Sorbet, 72

Mushrooms
Grilled Summer Vegetables, 72
Pita Pizzas, 82
Spring-Green Tortellini
    Salad, 33
Vegetable and Tofu Stir-Fry, 50

Nuts and Seeds
Almond-Pumpkin Muffins, 107
Apple-Nut Salad, 86
Cabbage-Apple Salad, 82
Chunky Apple and Peanut-
    Butter Cookies, 82
Dried Fruit and Nut
    Dressing, 106
Easy Whole-Wheat Bread With
    Sunflower Seeds, 93

Green Beans With Blue Cheese
    and Almonds, 56
Kay's Almond Drink, 102

Oatmeal
Apple-Pear Crisp, 97
Apricot-Raisin Bars, 88
Oatmeal Cookie
    Sandwiches, 102

Onion
Sweet Onion and Blended
    Cheese Pizza, 133
Sweet Onion–Potato Salad, 71

Orange
Carrot, Raisin, and Orange
    Salad, 50
Citrus-Banana Wake-up, 45
Citrus Medley, 128
50-50 Shake, 84
Marinated Avocado Salad, 121
Omelet Primavera, 43
Orange Cider, 127
Orange-Peach Frost, 136
Orange-Raspberry
    Vinaigrette, 24
Orange Sauce, 43

Papaya
Caribbean Quencher, 75

Pasta
Enchanted Forest Pasta, 37
Garden Pasta Salad, 71
Spinach-Tofu Lasagna, 111
Spring-Green Tortellini
    Salad, 33
Tropical Fruit Pasta, 30
Vegetable Stroganoff, 121

Peach
Berry-Peach Soup, 53
Fruit Salad, 52

Honey-Peach Bran Muffins, 18
Orange-Peach Frost, 136
Spiced Fruit Compote, 103

Peanut Butter
Chunky Apple and Peanut
    Butter Cookies, 82

Pear
Apple-Pear Crisp, 97
Fresh Fruit and Blue Cheese
    Salad, 133
Spiced Fruit Compote, 103

Peas
Good Earth Salad, 57
Spring Garden Vegetable
    Soup, 22
Sweet Pea Pod Soup, 15
Tofu–Snap Pea Salad, 66

Pineapple
Caribbean Quencher, 75
Fresh Fruit Kabobs, 39
Fresh Fruit Medley, 44
Fruit Salad, 52
Pineapple-Banana Slush, 121
Spiced Fruit Compote, 103
Tropical Fruit Pasta, 30
Tropical Strawberry Sherbet, 35

Potato
Cream of Potato and Watercress
    Soup, 130
Elegant Stuffed Potatoes, 140
Garden-Topped Potatoes, 66
Grilled Summer Vegetables, 72
Hearty Quick or Slow Stew, 115
Pumpkin and Potato Soup, 91
Spring Garden Vegetable
    Soup, 22
Sweet Onion-Potato Salad, 71
Sweet Potato Pancakes, 125
Two-Potato Twirls, 107
Whole-Wheat Potato Bread, 57

Protein
Complementary Proteins, 150

Pumpkin
Almond-Pumpkin Muffins, 107
Pumpkin and Potato Soup, 91

Raisin
Apricot-Raisin Bars, 88
Carrot, Raisin, and Orange
Salad, 50
Dried Fruit and Nut
Dressing, 106
Granola, 63
Raisin Sauce, 102

Raspberries
Berry-Banana Salad Mold, 103
Fresh Raspberry Yogurt, 68
Orange-Raspberry
Vinaigrette, 24
Raspberry Sauce, 119

Rice
Festive Broccoli-Topped
Holiday Rice, 137
Green Pepper Cups Stuffed
With Garden Vegetable
Pilaf, 96
Rice Acapulco, 75
Rice and Red Beans, 63
Vegetable and Tofu Stir-Fry, 50

Spinach
Artichoke-Spinach Bake, 100
Creamy Spinach Dip, 29
Spinach Salad, 98
Spinach-Tofu Lasagna, 111
Tender Spinach Crepes, 25
Tomato-Spinach-Mozzarella
Sandwiches, 89

Squash
Enchanted Forest Pasta, 37
Grilled Summer Vegetables, 72

Mexican Vegetables, 76
Pumpkin and Potato Soup in
Acorn Squash, 91
Summer Squash Soufflé, 56

Strawberry
Berry-Peach Soup, 53
Fresh Fruit Kabobs, 39
Fresh Fruit Medley, 44
Fresh Fruit Nestled in Barley
Salad, 25
Fruit Salad, 52
Layered Lemon Angel Dessert
and Strawberry Sauce, 26
Strawberry Sauce, 26
Sweetheart Strawberry
Mousse, 18
Tropical Strawberry Sherbet, 35

Sweet Potatoes
Sweet Potato Pancakes, 125
Two-Potato Twirls, 107

Tangerine
Citrus Medley, 128
Fresh Fruit Medley, 44

Tofu
Spinach-Tofu Lasagna, 111
Tofu-Honey Dressing, 86
Tofu–Snap Pea Salad, 66
Vegetable and Tofu Stir-Fry, 50

Tomato
Autumn Vegetable Soup, 97
Fresh Basil-Tomato Sauce, 25
Gazpacho Dip, 76
Grilled Summer Vegetables, 72
Herbed Parmesan
Tomatoes, 100
Marinara Sauce, 85
Minestrone Soup, 60
Pita Pizzas, 82
Spring Garden Vegetable
Soup, 22

Sun Country Tomato Salad, 67
Tomato Cocktail, 110
Tomato-Spinach-Mozzarella
Sandwiches, 89

Watercress
Cream of Potato and Watercress
Soup, 130
Watercress Dressing, 116

Whole Wheat
Dill Bread, 116
Easy Whole-Wheat Bread With
Sunflower Seeds, 93
Seven-Grain Cereal, 44
Whole-Wheat Potato Bread, 57
Whole-Wheat Scones, 111

Yogurt
Berry-Banana Salad Mold, 103
Creamy Cherry Dip, 39
Creamy Yogurt Topping, 52
Fresh Raspberry Yogurt in
Cookie Baskets, 68
Spiced Couscous in
Cantaloupe, 67
Yogurt-Cheese Frosting, 92
Yogurt-Cheese Spread, 139
Yogurt Dessert Sauce, 97

ABOUT THE THE AUTHOR

Karen Mangum is a Registered Dietitian and a seasoned recipe developer. Karen's recipes have appeared in numerous issues of Cooking Light Magazine, Cooking Light cookbooks and other national publications, including Famous Brand Name Recipes and Pillsbury's Fast and Healthy magazines. She is a member of the American Dietetic Association and received the Recognized Young Dietitian Award for the state of Idaho for her contributions to her profession.

Karen graduated from Brigham Young University with a master's degree in Clinical Nutrition and completed her internship at the University of Utah. She has had her own private practice for nearly 12 years, focusing on wellness education for groups and individuals. A few of her clients include Ore-Ida Foods, Weight Watchers International, Albertson's and Key Bank of Idaho.

Since 1990, Karen has educated thousands in her biweekly cooking and nutrition segments on the NBC affiliate's morning news program in Boise, Idaho. In addition, she is a popular cooking instructor at the Grand Gourmet Cooking School, specializing in "Light and Luscious" cuisine. Well known for her lively presentations and practical approach to fitness, Karen speaks often all across the country.

She has served as media representative for the American Dietetic Association and has appeared on numerous television and radio shows, including "CBS This Morning", "CNN On The Menu" and "Eye On Toronto".

Raised in Southern California, Karen now lives in Boise, Idaho, with her husband, Michael, and their four children where they enjoy the best of Idaho: river rafting, snow skiing and hiking.